POETRY NOW
SOUTHERN ENGLAND 2002

Edited by

Natalie Nightingale

First published in Great Britain in 2002 by
POETRY NOW
Remus House,
Coltsfoot Drive,
Peterborough, PE2 9JX
Telephone (01733) 898101
Fax (01733) 313524

HB ISBN 0 75432 726 4
SB ISBN 0 75432 727 2

FOREWORD

Although we are a nation of poets we are accused of not reading poetry, or buying poetry books. After many years of listening to the incessant gripes of poetry publishers, I can only assume that the books they publish, in general, are books that most people do not want to read.

Poetry should not be obscure, introverted, and as cryptic as a crossword puzzle: it is the poet's duty to reach out and embrace the world.

The world owes the poet nothing and we should not be expected to dig and delve into a rambling discourse searching for some inner meaning.

The reason we write poetry (and almost all of us do) is because we want to communicate: an ideal; an idea; or a specific feeling. Poetry is as essential in communication, as a letter; a radio; a telephone, and the main criterion for selecting the poems in this anthology is very simple: they communicate.

CONTENTS

The Tide	Eric W Baker	1
Late Summer Days	James W Bull	2
Upon A Pond	S Y Tarr	2
The Horseman	Michael Heath	3
. . . And The Living Is Easy!	Diana Crossman	4
Ionian Dawn	Michael N McKimm	4
All On A Summer's Evening	Gill Sathyamoorthy	5
Somerset Garden (Autumn)	Rosemary Langdon	6
The Visit	Monica Redhead	6
Past	Joey	7
A Drive Through Somerset	Margaret Smith	8
Osilla:	Angela Rodaway	9
Make Five Minutes	Mary Petrie	10
Changing Village Life	Mary Beale	11
Rose Of The West	Carolyn Fittall	12
Secret	Joanne Hale	13
Clouds	Joyce E Barrett	14
Eyes To Die For	Wendy Kellett	14
The Weir	Sue Duffy	15
Ode To A Barber	Mike Stowe	16
Wish Upon A Star	Lisa Clarke	16
Love Is . . .	Nicholas Garcia	17
The Road	Rosina Winiarski	18
Survival	J Ashford	19
The Coming Of The Night	Elizabeth Anandadeva	20
Living Circuit	Edna Holford	20
My Life's A Pleasant Highway	Nicholas Winn	21
Machine Made	James Kerr	22
A Watery Grave	Dora Watkins	22
Not Knowing	Margery Fear	23
The Castle Of St George - Lisbon	Sylvia Fairclough	24
Merry May	Joan Boswell	24
Yes, I Remember It Well	Eileen Witt-Way	25
Still Here	Emma Francis	26

Thought For The Day	Sheila Dodwell	26
Day's End	John Barr	27
A High Price?	C R Watkinson	28
I Wish For . . .	Ian Fisher	28
Dancin' Man	Cavan Magner	29
The Kingswood Miner	Dennis Brockelbank	30
For You	Joanne H Hale	31
A Borrowed Day	Judith Thomas	32
Hallowe'en	J M Stoles	32
Beyond The Clouds	Joyce Coghlan	33
Somerset Stars	Brian R Russ	34
The Alluring Aisles Of Sainsbury's	Sheila Burnett	35
Love's Magic	Joan Chapman	36
The Flower	Gill Watson	36
August Magic	Rosemary A V Sygrave	37
The Church Of Destiny	Edgar Wall	38
Bath Abbey Courtyard	Gwen Hoskins	39
Time Travel	Mark Tuck	40
Summer	Bubbles Gaynor	40
Why The Salamander?	Grace Gauld	41
Haymaking	Evelyn Westwood	42
The Royal British Legion	Gillian M Morphy	42
Sadness	D Parrott	43
The Butterfly	Lisa Bennett	44
Evening Star	S H Smith	44
Pathway To Heaven	Derek Pile	45
A Tesco Trolley's Lament	Barbara Watson	46
Cameos	Joyce Reeves Holloway	47
Dodo	Peter Gillott	48
Sign Of The Times	Bob White	49
Winning?	Christopher Hayward	50
Oh! To Be Famous!	Christina R Maggs	50
The Stranger	Sylvia Connor	51
The Weather In The Streets	John Brackenbury	52
Feelings For Peter	Kim Brogan	52
My Next Summer Holiday	Keith Lainton	53
Perpetual Motion	Roma Davies	54

Yesterday's Child	J M Armstead	55
Cosy	M Wood	56
We'll Miss You Meg	Sarah Linsdell	56
A Godly Soldier	R J Collins	57
Ripples On The Water	Licia Johnston	58
Afterwards	Frank Ede	58
Let There Be Peace	Marie Croucher	59
Forbidden Love	Bahar	60
Opposites	Linda Hughes	60
My Tale Of Love	Kenneth Matthews	61
The Day The World Went Mad	Debbie Barnard	62
Season's Dawn	A Starbuck	63
My Nan	Patricia Heath	64
Leaving Home	Elizabeth Morton	64
Contemplation	Michelle Quinton-Jarvis	65
Show Jumping At Hickstead	Gladys C'Ailceta	66
Thoughts	T C Hollis	66
Ask	Anouska Louise Aitkenhead	67
England	Constance Pugh	68
Tunnel Vision	Harry Higginson	69
A Poet's Highway	Howard Thorn	70
The Burning Bush	Dave Davis	70
The Girl From Amsterdam	Anthony Michael Doubler	71
Untitled	Phyllis O'Connell (Hampson)	72
Faith In Life	Mary Biggs	72
Are You Waiting?	S D Rose	73
Mr Ant	James Barry	74
Faerie	Pam Hammocks	74
Motherhood	Maggie Fairbrace	75
Trapped	Lorna Young	76
Valley View (Inspired By The Wye Valley)	Ann Voaden	77
Fat Cats	Ed King	78
Seasonal Cycle Of Nature	Paul Mynard	79
I Promised The Wind	Susan E Roffey	80
Intensive Care	Dennis Cohen	80
English Weather	K M Inglis-Taylor	81
The Jersey Battle Of Flowers	Mabel Helen Underwood	82

Bygone Brighton	Jonathan Bryant	83
A Moment In Guadalajara	Rex Baker	84
The Path	Pippa Suggett	84
Seagulls	Beryl R Daintree	85
Wiston Springs	David Tas	86
Don't	Lyndsey Power	86
Follow Thy Guide	Josephine Foreman	87
Autumn	Judith Garrett	88
The Blarney Stone	Leonard T Coleman	88
The Power Of The Invisible	Sylvia Gwilt	89
Knowlege And Wisdom	Maurice Webb	90
In New Park Road, Chichester	Michael Rowson	90
September Morning	Hilary Moore	91
Louise Of Cornwall	David de Pinna	92
On Receipt Of A 50th Birthday Card	Sue Morley	93
Lone Wolf	Danny Coleman	94
A Good Cigar	Derek Marshall	94
Life Of Glass	Veronica Charlwood Ross	95
Pretending	Laura Edwards	96
The Gulls From The Sea	Meryl Champion	96
The Closed Door	Michael Wilson	97
Freedom	G Poole	98
A Family Portrait	Les D Pearce	98
Dream What You Will	Rosemary Watts	99
Awareness	Suzanne Joy Golding	100
Unburied Treasure	Bee Kenchington	100
Guardian Angel	Jennifer Hayes	101
Bus Stop	Pete Simmons	102
August	E M Apps	102
Summer Scene	Pete Bauer	103
Water	Pamela Jennings	103
The Freedom Of Release	Angela R Davies	104
Golden Jubilee - Pride In A Nation	Lorna Tippett	104
Cherish	Michael Alan Fenton	105
Ode To Wild Parsley	Edith Buckeridge	106
Harvest Morning	Clive A Baldwin	107

Loved And Lost	Kate Sorby	108
Words	Geoff Hume	108
To The Child In Me	Norah Green	109
Circadian Rhythm	Jeanne Walker	110
Think Very Carefully	Josie Lawson	111
I Can't Sleep	Deborah Carol Hughes	112
Hive	Jim Wilson	113
A Thatched Cottage In Selsey	Karen Grover	114
The Cat In Autumn	S R Hawk'sbee	114
A Villanelle	Frances Burrow	115
Tea With Aunt Laura	Catherine Curtis	116
Springtime	Rhona Cooper	116
Heir Of Hope And Glory	Cyril Skeet	117
Skyscrapers Die In Flames	Sheila Rowland	118
Avoiding The Light	Derek Blackburn	119
The Mount	J Eastaugh	120
The Meaning Of Life	Lindsey Brown	120
Summer Is Glorious	Linda Webster	121
Truly Free	Denise Shaw	122
My Love For You	Annette Harold	122
Snowfall	G Howarth	123
In Care	Alan Millard	123
The Neighbour's Cat	Doreen M Bowers	124
Crab Apples	Anita E Dye	125
Summer Postcards	A K S Shaw	126
Granny's Picture	Phyllis Wright	127
The War Room	Paul Willis	128
The Saddest Spring	Joan Hopkins	128
The Spear Carrier's Apprentice	Dai Blatchford	129
Grandad	Kayleigh Rhodes	130
The Rufus Stone	Maud Eleanor Hobbs	131
The Star Princess	Charles F H Ruddick	132
Chance To Believe	Steve Wright	132
Embrace Of The Sea	Moyle Breton	133
Cornish Coasts	Lucy Bloxham	134
September 2001	Phil McLynn	134
River Dream	Olive Wright	135
Cornish Sanctuary	Ann Linney	136

Time - Howarth Car Park	Hilary Jean Clark	137
The Sounds Of Cornwall	Paddy Jupp	138
One Less Tomorrow	Pat Heppel	138
A Relative	M MacDonald-Murray	139
Ode To Topsy	Kate Laity	140
Greetings Yellow	T Webster	141
Born In Devon	Evelyn Scott Brown	142
Being There	Jeremy J Croucher	142
Wild November Night	Molly Rodgers	143
While It's Warm	Andy Botterill	144
The Greater Light	Diana Momber	145
On The Moor	Anne Lawry	146
The White Goose	Martin Norman	146
The Madness Of Pain	Trudi James	147
Penwith	Jinty Knowling Lentier	147
While The Seed Sings	Sheila Jeffries	148
Afternoon On Dartmoor	Peg Ritchie	148
Cool Soft Shade Of Polished Rags	Simon Brown	149
Untitled	M Pellow	150
The Birth Of An Opal	Marion Susan Cornbill	151
Emerald Eyes	Danielle Collins	152
If	Ela Fleming	152
City Oasis	Sheila J Holmes	153
Dancers	Sullivan	154
Precious	J Snowsill	155
Birds	Linda Young	156
Some Things You Never Get Over	Geoffrey Downton	156
Always There	Jeannette Jackson	157
Rock Pool	Diana H Adams	158
Commons Time	V Jean Tyler	159
A Friendship	Patricia Evans	160
The Transformation	Clare Allen	160
The Millennium Bobby	K Cook	161
My Awareness	Anthony Ross-Fallon	162
Friendship	Pam Stevens	162

Outback Painter's Composition	Janine Vallor	163
Evenings Over The Isles Of Scilly	Gerald Conyngham	164
Raymond	Phyllis Ing	165
Reviewing The Situation	Wendy Watkin	166
Beauty	Enid Gill	167
The Winds Of Time	Jenny Proom	168
Fossil Forest At Lulworth	Kathleen M Hatton	169
Cup Of Love	Brenda Weir	170
Always The Woods	Chris White	170
You And I	D Marriott	171
Nelly	Phillip A Taylor	172
An Open Book	Lynn Shakespeare Branner	172
What Is Age?	Muriel Johnson	173
A Shackled Sonnet	Jack Major	174
Christchurch	Betty Green	174
11th September 2001	Catherine Blackett	175
Youth	C L Buchanan-Brown	175
Never Again	Hollie Simmons	176
Snake	Kathleen Harper	176
Poole Wind Sprites	Di Bagshawe	177
A Lower Latitude	Laura Lang	178
Restless Byways	Robert Newland	178
Now There Is One	Yvonne Lewis	179
The Dancing	P Henderson	180
August Holiday	Janet Eirwen Smith	181
Decision Time	Will A Tilyard	182
Shadows Of Autumn	Grace Anderson	183
The America's Cup Jubilee	Norah Page	184
Leave Only Footprints	Ann Marie Moseley	185
Science	Desmond Tarrant	186
The A30 In Springtime	John Jenkin	186
Flight	Georgina McManus	187
On The Wind	Ted Harriott	188
Time That Passes	John Amsden	189
Hush Little Baby	Jenny Brownjohn	190

THE TIDE

(A Quamina)

The tide advances, then recedes,
And naught her measured tread impedes,
For sun and moon dictate the motion
Of ev'ry sea and ev'ry ocean.

The tide advances, then withdraws
From regal cliffs and sand-strewn shores.
Unknowing, meeting mankind's needs,
The tide advances, then recedes.

The tide advances, then retreats.
No obstacle her aim defeats.
Her mission unchanged, without pause,
The tide advances, then withdraws.

The tide advances, then retires,
And, in her motion, she inspires
Poets to idyllic feats.
The tide advances, then retreats.

The tide advances, then subsides,
And tribute to her none derides.
Oblivious of man's vain desires,
The tide advances, then retires.

The tide advances, then recedes,
Unruffled by man and his deeds.
Whate'er it is mankind decides
The tide advances, then subsides.

Eric W Baker

LATE SUMMER DAYS

The miles behind as the bike ride ends
A glass, the garden, soon dusk descends
Thinking about my town again
In these late summer days

The river moves, waterfowl sleep
There're football shouts and sounds on streets
The pulsing pub has empty seats
In these late summer days

The swifts stay high, doves rest in trees
Church bells mingle with the breeze
The so slow turning of the leaves
Here in late summer days

And after how the weeks have been
Scorching by day, a warm evening scene
And now those all become a dream
Into late summer days

So the first star introduces night
Before the last wash of pale sunlight
And rests the soul in a peaceful sight
End of late summer days.

James W Bull

UPON A POND

I came upon a sparkling pond,
With water lilies all abloom,
Insects were flying through the reeds
That rustled in the wind beyond.

A kingfisher dived from some height,
While the frog sat on his lily pad and croaked,
It watched keeping his breakfast in full sight.

A grass snake slithered through the weeds,
That parted and swayed with movement that
Silently dispersed their precious seeds.

The water glistened in the sun,
Dragonflies stepped across the glassy surface
And rested on the leafy edge,
Until the day was done.

S Y Tarr

THE HORSEMAN

Through sage and chaparral we'll go,
With heads held high, with stirrup low.
Past burning rock and granite tor,
Where mighty mountain rivers roar.

Over ancient mountain's snowy head
Into sunsets painted crimson red,
With flying mane and flying tail,
With golden sun on golden trail.

Through cloudless days and moonlit nights,
Through fiery plains and rock-strewn heights,
Past eagle's nest and wild-cat lair,
Where vultures sweep the rising air.

Through icy winds and driven snow,
Through lightning strike and hammer blow,
Into forests dark as deepest night,
That yields to nought but campfire light.

And when my earthly trails are done,
Lay me close to where wild mountain rivers run;
Go place a cross by yonder tree,
For hereabouts a man with horse ran free.

Michael Heath

. . . AND THE LIVING IS EASY!

Summer do not leave us yet!
Scarlet and yellow crocosmia
Scorch the eyes and lead us down
To heavy-petalled dahlias, candy-pink,
Curly fronds lie on the emerald grass.
Light drifts of lavender
A haven for the bees that buzz about
In honey-drenched bliss.
Between cascades of orange and russet-red
Are prim and stalky daisies
Making contrasts of colour even brighter.
More blobs of orange
Made by the marigolds
That hug the soil.
Godetias now turning brown,
The breeze ripples the garden flames
Not time for autumn yet!

Diana Crossman

IONIAN DAWN

Awakening slowly
to a perfect dawn.
The wind abated in
the darkness.

The raging foam flecked sea
of yesterday.
A Herculean millpond
gently caressing the stilled
sand of the shore.

Distant islands so clear
in the storm.
Lost in the promising
heat haze of this
new day.

Michael N McKimm

ALL ON A SUMMER'S EVENING

The sun has set
The lamp lights are burning
The garden quiet after a busy day
And yet still warm from the hot sun's ray.

The incense is lit
The fountain is trickling
Sweet music is playing
And candles in the garden are flickering.

Hearts and minds are calmed
Eyes close, lips are smiling,
Thoughts of fine friendships that last
And thankfulness for the good things present and past.

The still night air
The dark blue sky
Suddenly reveals pink clouds above -
Magical moments on the wings of a dove.

Flames are dancing
Sweet aromas are drifting
Memories shared and burdens eased,
All on a summer's evening, peace received.

Gill Sathyamoorthy

SOMERSET GARDEN (AUTUMN)

Autumn is not mellow in this garden,
Bright berries warn of coming cool days
Fleshy stemmed begonias, much burdened
By huge flaming blooms, brazenly raise
Gaudy heads curving over wooden tubs,
Fuchsias shower powerfully out of pots,
Reds and purples predominate, to rub
Shoulders and clash with violently hot
Orange montbretias on raised bank above,
(Planning needs a measure of aplomb!)
And even further back buddleias shove
Mauve shoots centre stage, fading blossom
Attracting butterflies, ignored by cat
Stretched out on warm border - disdaining
Also chattering gorging starlings that
Strip elder fruit - nothing remaining
But summer dusty leaves, its ancient arms
Twisted with time, underneath promise
Of the primrose seedling's pale petalled charms,
Hope of spring and harsh winter's demise.

Rosemary Langdon

THE VISIT

The participants approach, footsteps gently gliding,
hearts leap sickeningly, pale melancholy
faces strain with painful humour,
the undertow of love surfaces fleetingly.

The waiter hovers, smile assumed, mask of expectation,
celebratory meats support stuffed appetites,
hands poise, teeth gleam, lips move avidly,
the quartet strives with unusual amity.

The countryside extends with swelling curves,
soft fronded trees and clustered cattle,
the walk commences, wild flowers bestrew wild streams
the senses lurk sensuously, lie constrainedly.

An empty room, unstructured linen,
conglomerate of litter loitered in, beds made love in,
the massed imagined hurts of childhood quiver,
a longingness arises for indivisibility.

Monica Redhead

PAST

Stones at Stonehenge
Will always remain
But most things we had
We won't see again.
The towns that were busy
Engulfed in smoke
Leaving their trail of coal dust and smoke
Chimney sweeps working to keep chimneys clean
A familiar sight, no more to be seen.
Hawthorn hedges, wooden gates and stiles
Countless green fields
That stretched out for miles
Navvies leaning upon their shovels
Office girls sitting reading their novels
Screaming trams and the baker's cart
In early hours they had to depart.
And ancient pubs with 'ye olde names',
Things will never be the same again.
No more signs saying 'less expense'
'Nothing in these stores, costing more than six pence'.
For today's modern people, this doesn't seem grand
But to me it was great - it was my old England.

Joey

A DRIVE THROUGH SOMERSET
*(Dedicated to a ride through the Somerset countryside
with Margaret Gilder)*

There is blossom in abundance
As you drive along the lanes and byways
Of Somerset on a sunny morning in May;
Glastonbury Tor is just visible through the haze,
Cattle are munching the grass in nearby fields,
You can feel the warmth of the sun shining
through the windscreen,
The bare winter landscape is almost forgotten.

Leafy glades nestle between the farms,
A cow is scratching its nose on a bush,
Ancient monuments litter the countryside,
Some in disrepair.
Sheep wool sticks to the hedgerows
Small churches are dotted over the landscape
Standing proudly as they have done for centuries.

Driving through the wetlands
Moorhens dart hither and thither on the withy covered rhines,
Otters are visible for keen eyes to see,
Swans swimming in stately fashion with their cygnets,
The sensitive twitching of a vole's nose peeps out of the bulrushes,
Honeycombed stacks of peat are viewed in nearby fields.

Driving back through the villages with their soft,
ham stone cottages,
There is a colourful carpet of bluebells swaying in the wind
And wagtails with their tails dipping up and down,
are visible on the banks nearby.
Celandines and stately flags cover the fields
Interspersed with little clumps of trees.

In the heartland of Somerset stands Glastonbury -
The Isle of Avalon,
Where paganism fights against the early Christian beliefs,
Peoples come here in search of God - the true God?
Kindle in us a burning flame of love for the true God!
Somerset is all things to all men.

Margaret Smith

OSILLA:
(Great Ormond Street Hospital For Children 2001)

Once I sang to a crying child, a babe in arms
whose eyes as I sang met mine
till the crying became singing.

Do not let them die
those armed men in Kosovo
remember an eye for an eye
and do not let them die.

Osilla!
She and you were combined in a trinity
and you had knowledge, before you were born,
of the boot and the fist and the rifle butt.
Will your soft limbs that stiffen and shake
now ever move joyfully?

Your father, thin faced and onyx-eyed
gently drips your mother's milk
into the tube passed through your baby nose

You have a voice (they call it 'vocalisation')
but you do not cry. Can you cry?
Can blinded eyes weep?
And if I sing will you sing with me?

Angela Rodaway

MAKE FIVE MINUTES

If the sun shines today, make five minutes.
Go to a remote spot and find a flower - a daisy will do.
Really concentrate on it.
It was there yesterday before you found it.
It will still be there when you leave it.

If the sky is clear tonight, make five minutes.
Look up and find a star - any star will do.
Really concentrate on it.
It was there before you saw it.
It will be there tomorrow, even if clouds cover it.

If you can get away tonight, make five minutes.
Believe that God is with you.
He was there yesterday, even if you didn't speak to him.
He will be there tomorrow, even if you don't praise him.

He made that flower (and all the others).
He made that star (and all the others).
He made the whole world - and he made you, too.
Isn't it time to thank him for making flowers and stars,
        for being there
        and for loving you?

Open the lines of communication now.
Tomorrow you'll be glad that you did . . .
        make five minutes.

Mary Petrie

CHANGING VILLAGE LIFE

Try to ignore the oncoming traffic noise
Lean hard into the hedgerow for safety's sake
Imagine a time when men wore corduroys
Toiled for estate owner with scythe and rake.
Carried goods to the market by horse and cart
Eggs, home-made butter and cream were the wives' perk.
Special clothes kept for occasions to look smart,
Skilled local craftsmen took great pride in their work.

Some children walked miles to the village school
Picked flowers or wild strawberries on the way.
Good behaviour in the classroom was the rule
Eyes closed, heads bowed, for others they learnt to pray.
Life had a rhythm, governed by each season
Sowing, planting, sheep shearing, reaping, storing.
People helped out without question or reason
A sense of community that was the thing.

In six or seven decades times changed indeed,
Farms are now worked in a business like manner
Livestock details computerised - healthy breed.
Veg and fruit frozen or sent to the canner.
A wide range of subjects are taught at school
Parents commute to work by car, all dressed smart
Words have different meanings like wicked or cool.
But nature still plays her unstoppable part.

Mary Beale

ROSE OF THE WEST

Rose of the West
Golden and true
Lighting the skies
With eyes so blue

A lady of such
Joy and charm
Who could ever
Wish her harm

The warmest smile
A gentle laugh
She went to God
On her garden path

Lost in an instant
On an ordinary day
Beautiful Jill
Stolen away

The West remembers
This beautiful girl
We will not forget
Weston's pearl

Walk in Jill's garden
Planted with love
For our golden angel
In heaven above.

Carolyn Fittall

SECRET

I look from my window
The moon is shining bright
Everywhere is calm
On this warm summer's night
The stars are sparkling
The night is hazy
People are sleepy
Tired and lazy
Contentment on faces
Of old and young
Skin slightly burning
From the afternoon sun
Creatures are active
They thrive in the dark
I walk through the trees
Carve my name in the bark
I smile to myself
Happiness is all around
I giggle with pleasure
Of the place I have found
Only I know it's there
It is my secret place
Over the bridge I see the river
Reflecting back my own face
This is where I long to be
Where everything is fine
Do you know where it is?
Of course not - because it's mine.

Joanne Hale

CLOUDS

White clouds drifting across the sky
Their beauty seen as they drift by.
In different shapes they wend their way,
Hiding the sun on a summer's day.
If one watches one can see
Pictures that change incessantly.
And in the sky on a stormy day,
The clouds are black as they wend their way.
Shading the earth against the sun
To bring us rain to spoil our fun.
And as the evening closes day
The clouds are edged with a golden ray.
All clouds are different, and all have names
There's a beauty in all for they're never the same.

Joyce E Barrett

EYES TO DIE FOR

Caught in the glare
Of eyes like these -
Lamps to light
You to deep
Darkness.
Owls of shadow
Owls of stealth,
Owling in the night.
Feathered silence.
Eyes to die for
Eyes like these.

Wendy Kellett

THE WEIR

Swishing, splashing sounds,
Swirl in and out of the languishing boughs,
That stoop to touch the waters of the weir.

A place of turmoil,
Sensed long before the foaming flecks of water
Catch the eye and stir the imagination.

Stand and gaze,
As the quiet stream that feeds the weir
Drifts slowly through the lush green fields,
Gently caressing the banks of overhanging grass.

Watch, as swiftly the waters gather speed
Rushing headlong towards the slime green steps,
Over which it hurls itself with unrelenting passion.

Listen, to the thunderous roar that resounds in the air,
As the waters crash and tumble
In a madness of white foam-flecked fury.

Wonder, at the rainbow coloured mist
That shimmers like a myriad of bright jewels,
As the tiny beads of water jostle and dance
On the edge of the watery precipice.

Stare, at the seething, white whirlpool of water
As it swirls and splashes,
Eagerly forcing the ripples of foam to wash the banks of the weir.

Sue Duffy

ODE TO A BARBER

Remember that we're British chaps
and keep the upper lip profoundly stiff.

Let barbers have the right to strike,
be glad that hair cream may yet quell the factory whiff.

What would the world be, once bereft of gay shampoo?
For chemists may sell toothpaste, and hardware merchants, glue
and only a placid continuity renew!

This democracy that numbs the brain,
sets fashion free to direct and train, the sad unwary.
But barbers are philosophers . . .
and have sworn to serve the hairy!

Let us with anarchists, now join in unity,
just for a season, for a while.
To break the dreariness of this democracy . . .
let barbers lead us with their ever friendly smile!

For politics, and mathematics, weave a web of complicated logic.
Oh barbers, snip it with your scissors, and let the light shine through!
And comb the hair of every democrat forever,
And comb the hair of every rebel too!

Mike Stowe

WISH UPON A STAR

When I wish upon a star.
The one I see from afar.
I wish for happiness and glee.
I wish away the evil in me.
I wish for good to overcome bad.
I wish that people wouldn't be sad.
I wish for the whole world to know, that I do love it so.

Someone's just died from hunger and greed.
Some people have money so they can eat.
There's war and evil cursing this land.
God will help us if He can.
So when you wish upon a star,
Makes no difference who you are.
Just remember the things I've said.
Put bad and evil out of your head.

Lisa Clarke

LOVE IS . . .

Love is bleak, enigmatic
Devouring the mind's elation,
Bonding for a revolution,
Fighting for inner evolution.

But still too weak to soothe starvation.

Love is an alcoholic nectar
The mighty emperor of emotions
The infinite goddess of sensations
A holy taste of liberation
An ever-pure scented raindrop in descent,
A blooming flower,
Heaven sent.

Love is a seed on infertile land
A seething journey of diverse thoughts.
A death defying pilgrim,
Woven with addiction.
A bible I seek,
Of dwindling fiction
But as I forage through mist
Of spiralling renditions
I realise that love is a sad apparition.

Nicholas Garcia (14)

THE ROAD

Road
A long, thin ribbon
Stretching ahead
Seemingly forever.
It loses itself in the distance
Where a line of hazy blue hills
Are blurred into an Exmoor sky.
I am on top of the world
As I speed along
With the bracing air
Playfully whipping my hair.
However far I travel
The same horizon is always there
Teasingly ahead.
The same endless rows of beech
Line the route
And tall, spear-headed flowers
Stand to attention like purple sentinels:
Familiar landmarks flash past.
I am alone in this place of grandeur,
Alone with the land and the sky.
From somewhere high in space
I must look like an ant
Crawling across a vast, unwritten page.
Perhaps the hills are a mirage
And the road an illusion
Which leads finally
To nowhere -
And -
Everywhere.

Rosina Winiarski

SURVIVAL

Can she survive
Despite the distress
My answer is
Yes

Tears have been shed
A heart has bled
Loved ones have flown
Am I
Alone

Courage is fame
Fighting on, the game
Life will never be the
Same

Would you agree
If one were to see
This spirit is strong
For I will live
On

Read my words
Again and again
Have you felt
The incredible
Pain

Can you admit
That I haven't quit
I will climb out
Of this bottomless
Pit.

J Ashford

THE COMING OF THE NIGHT

Sun fades from
The still fields;
Light eases from
The land as night
Falls, and greyness
Fills the evening sky
As it merges into night's
Enfolding womb of blackness.
Hidden the whole day long
Stars sparkle one by one,
Until in their thousands,
The sky is splattered with
Twinkling lights awakening
The soul to ponder on worlds
And universes beyond this
Little planet softly glowing
Out in space 'midst countless
Other stars and planets;
And for a while one is lost
In wonder at so many lights.

Elizabeth Anandadeva

LIVING CIRCUIT

Let Divine Love flow through me
nor ever let there be
any obstacle to hinder its
radiating influence around me.

Let its magnetic healing power
attract those seeking souls who need
to feel and share this boundless love
in thought and word and deed

Let Creative Love move through each and all,
from group to group let it circulate
and radiate, magnetise and - celebrate
the inner-outer structure of the one inclusive whole.

Edna Holford

MY LIFE'S A PLEASANT HIGHWAY

My life's a pleasant highway
Which I coast along at leisure,
With welcome views to grace the way
That bring me joy and pleasure:
I wind the windows of my mind
As far down as they'll go
To let the breeze of living in
To keep my heart aglow:

The only thing I know that lends
My life a touch of sadness
Is sensing that not all my friends
Can share my glimpse of gladness:
And knowing too, that though my view
On life is clear and pleasing,
So many people passing through
Find grief and gloom, uneasing:

I'm thankful for the route I take,
So pleasant every mile:
For all its cheering sights which make
My soul content and smile:
I'll cruise on, grateful I can thrive
On simple fuels to fire me,
Like love and happiness which drive
My spirit and inspire me.

Nicholas Winn

MACHINE MADE

A dream flicks through the mind of the young
The rainbow smiles from above a race has begun
For pots of gold lie at ends of rainbows they've been told, they believe
Thinking not of what they possess but of what they can achieve.

Hope is a word riddled with lies
For hope comes from suffering behind a disguise
Life is a race, not with rainbows but with yourself
And hope can creep up on you with surprise and with stealth.

But like lemmings on clifftops we run for the light
Not looking for danger, not willing to fight
And like many before us we fall to the floor
We lie helpless there on the trap door.

Soon we will fall further into the dark
The light in your eyes has gone we have lost the spark
Because life is in your hands my friend and your hands, they are tied
And down is where you're heading, your hope has just died.

And so once more we all become slaves
All sugar-coated, pre-packed and weighed
We will be forgotten, no wreaths will be laid
For the truth is we are all machine made.

James Kerr

A WATERY GRAVE

Aeons ago, the sea lapped the tor
Leaving large lakes, where now is moor
Where the monks took out their boats to fish
For making many a tasty dish.

Centuries later the moors were drained
Acres of land were then reclaimed
Farmers summered their cattle there then
Forgetting days from way back when.

Now global warming may higher tides
Breaching the sea defences wide
Summer county may be no more
With sea, rushing, through every door.

Dora Watkins

Not Knowing

Why do those thoughts just drift away
and stay outside my mind.
Who can I ask, what would they say
- what answers might I find?

What are those words I strain to hear
that voice I should have known.
Why do I feel a friend is near
- when I am so alone?

Whose dim reflection stares and cries
whose tears that fall with mine.
It's not a face I recognise
- or was there once a time?

Is this a feeling I once knew
this pounding of my heart.
I thought I gave them all to you
- or were they torn apart?

Whose is the face that hovers there
I try so hard to see.
Are you someone who used to care
- was there a you and me?

Margery Fear

THE CASTLE OF ST GEORGE - LISBON

Arches, parapets and doors
Dream in a high blue sky
Lulled by sun and flowers
In the castle of the Moors.

Watery-mouthed fountains in wall and square
Sun rinse the hours, here where I sit
On marble bench screen-scented by the rose
Here where the scarlet bougainvillea
Tumbles down worn and haunted steps.

Aloof white peacocks with gold guinea fowl
Delicately pace the gritty paths.
Silently shake and shudder then preen and bow
Their feathery cloaks raising a regal brow.

Arches, parapets and doors
Dream in a high blue sky
Safe both the coiling sea and precious city
Still guarded by the Moors.

Sylvia Fairclough

MERRY MAY

Where the maypole stands
On village green
The children dance and
Intertwine the coloured ribbons
Back and forth, and to and fro
The music stops, they bow
Disperse, and run off into the cow parsley
Queen Anne's lace, their laughter says.

Joan Boswell

YES, I REMEMBER IT WELL

The day my sister was born
I remember it well.
No lights or candles and only three
I remember it well.
Being took to Gran's, I wanted Mum
I remember it well.
The rabbit stew and Sunday roast
I remember it well.
Dad cutting the grass, making the hay
I remember it well.
The smell of strong cider, I felt sick
I remember it well.
Dad and Mum, milking all by hand
I remember it well.
The froth on top of the churn
I remember it well.
The smell of washing in the old copper
I remember it well.
Turning that mangle, I'll never forget
I remember it well.
Hanging from apple tree, calico knicks'
I remember it well.
Christmas cake and puddings, Mum's mince pies
I remember it well.
Two small socks Christmas morning
I remember it well.
First run up the garden to the loo
I remember it well.
The bonfire that caught the hedge afire
I remember it well.
Memories of childhood never fade
Yes, I remember them well.

Eileen Witt-Way

STILL HERE

Memories remain,
Photographs remind,
Your face constantly in my life;
My path of direction across the river,
Guilt and regrets pass with time.
So much time has passed,
Many things have changed.
You are still part of me,
Your voice grows in me,
Tears roll, happy thoughts,
Still denying what has happened;
Doubting that you have gone,
Blocking out the fear of no return.
We must move on;
Learn to let go, look to the future,
Celebrate and enjoy what we had,
But move on with our lives.
Accept what has happened,
Accept the next step,
They would support your judgement,
Don't wish what could have been,
Look forward, not back.

Emma Francis

THOUGHT FOR THE DAY

Truth's no longer eternal,
Nor evil bad.
Honesty's a weakness,
No time to feel sad.

Morality's meaningless,
Caring out of date.
Responsibility's a failing
Regret will come too late.

Let's win the lottery,
To hell with the rest.
Plan only for ourselves,
The way we know best.

All seems lost,
But should we despair?
Shake off this gloom
And pluck hope from the air!

Sheila Dodwell

DAY'S END

It is early evening,
the day is nearly done.
Sitting in the garden,
in the evening sun.

Enjoying the peace and a quiet moment,
watching the clouds roll by.
The clouds looking like balls of wool,
I sit thinking of the miracles in the sky.

Strong winds are blowing,
the leaves making a rustling sound.
Tree branches bending over,
nearly touching the ground.

It is late in the evening,
and the sun has almost gone down.
Now the sun is behind the sky line
casting shadows on the ground.

It has now become dark,
the houses full of light.
It is the end of the day,
now it has become the night.

John Barr

A HIGH PRICE?

Deep, deep below, beneath acres of earth dug dirt,
Scores of men in ten-hour shifts would work.
To toil and labour every minute of every working day
Bringing home a much needed but alas meagre pay.
Before the dawn and into darkness a cage would
disappear and descend
Only to emerge much later when daylight had come to
its end.
Grown men crawled around tunnels pitch black and
running with damp,
With only a yellow glow from a pale flickering helmet lamp.
Mid-day the toil would cease and numerous snap tins would open
A lunchtime repast when bread could be broken.
The men ignored the rats that to and fro scurried,
Only if the canary breathed its last - would they stop and worry?
Too often the seams overhead had to take the weight
Strain for the dug out earth - was far too great.
The earth gave out, one last protesting sound
Before she buried - those brave men deep underground.

C R Watkinson

I WISH FOR . . .

The passion of an artist.
The wit of the comedian.
The emotions of an actor.
The story of a writer.

The cherished smile of a child.
The strength of a mother.
The forgiveness of a friend.
The trust of a father.

The soulful eyes of a lover.
The temper of a caged animal.
The charisma of a conman.
The calmness of a cleric.

Ian Fisher

DANCIN' MAN

Wanna be one?
Give it a whirl.
Don't need any Ginger,
You're a solo, man.

Follow famous feet
Of the past:
On a glass-like floor
Or in the rain.
Be a 'Bojangles'
Or a Tommy Roll.

So put on them
Dancin' shoes:
Rehearse an' curse,
Swing it, wing it,
Swirl it, twirl it,
Slide an' glide,
Slap it, tap it,
Storm it, perform it.

Blood an' sweat perfection
In syncopated rhythm,
Now you're a dancin' man,
Yeah.

Cavan Magner

THE KINGSWOOD MINER
(Kingswood Near Bristol)

In Kangs'ood in they olden days thee'd find
The whole area'l for jet black coal, was mined.
In thic there days I telt thee, times were really rough.
And Kangs'ood miners were, the toughest of the tough.

The hardest of em all, a burly man, called Joe,
Had reputation, known so far and wide, thee's know.
The tons of coal he shovelled, to earn a little more.
Just went into yon landlord's hand, inside the tavern door.

For, no man was better at roistering than 'E'.
But spare a thought, dear friend, for his poor family.
No poorer home thee'd find wherever thee'ud search,
No furniture, so wife and childer, had nowhere to perch.

Then came the day, the glory day, we though ud never be.
The missioner Charles Wesley came, from sin set our Joe free.
What a change of life took place, tood reely make 'E' laugh.
His old pals of his rampaging just thought that 'E' be daft.

Saying 'Do 'E' reely think, the water changed to wine?'
'Dursn't know about that' he said, 'but summat I know fine,
My wife and childer now will have, a better life for sure.
For now I'm changing yonder beer, into furniture!'

That Kangs'ood home now hears the sound of merry childer lafter
This story ends the way it should. Just happy ever after.

Dennis Brockelbank

FOR YOU

If I could be
    Somewhere with you
All alone
    Just we two

What would we say?
    Things would be bliss
Feelings we would share
    I would not want to miss

We will walk along
    Looking at the sea
Silent, we may dream
    Of things that may be

Whispering to each other
    Again and again
Hand in hand, laughing
    As we walk in the rain

We would be together
    Everything will be fine
A question I would ask
    Will you ever be mine?

Yes, if I were
    Somewhere with you
Would you ask me
    The same question too?

Joanne H Hale

A Borrowed Day

A borrowed day impedes the force of rite;
Take hold, make space, cop out, recant, secede
Your bond with time; forget old rules, ignite
The blaze of glorious chance, don't bleed,
Life's blood runs out. Beware the sands of time,
The axe is gone, the noose made spare, escape
Unwieldy speed. What if we stand sublime
Refusing to commit? Prove virtue mere red tape!
Ignore past law, no good will come from there;
Walk straight away; get out of sight, elsewhere.
For when you've left no memory remains,
No recompense from burgeoning past chains.

Judith Thomas

HALLOWE'EN
(For Jean Parker)

In the dead of night
by the candlelight
a witch sits all alone
snakes and spiders
frogs and toads
and other insects by the load
into her cauldron
they all go
as she weaves her wicked
spells around you

The witches brew
is bad for you.

J M Stoles

BEYOND THE CLOUDS

'Beyond the clouds the sun is always shining'
Beyond the clouds that veil our heavenward gaze
We see but dimly through earth's misty vapours
The joys of Heaven prepared for future days.

Above the clouds of care and earthly sorrow
Above the clouds of toil and human woe,
Could we but see, God's perfect will is working
To bring us to the land where we would go.

Lord, be with us throughout our earthly journey
However dark and rough may be the way
While we have You, our precious Elder Brother
We know that we are safe from day to day.

Sometimes we wonder why our heavenward journey
Must lead through sad and lonely ways
But when we stand and see where God has led us
We know that He has planned out all our days.

You said 'Bear one another's burdens
Weep with the one who weeps.'
How could we fully understand that message
If we had never known life's hidden deeps.

We know Your way is best, although we murmur
Sometimes when we lose sight of Your dear face
Give us Your peace and walk beside us, Jesus
Keep us in paths of right, by Your own grace.

Joyce Coghlan

SOMERSET STARS

Fair traveller from afar
South Western bound,
Make Somerset your star
There's much to be found.

Linger at ease
And soak the atmosphere,
It's bound to please
Wherever you appear.

Roam over Exmoor
Where forest meets the sea,
Wookey Hole is a must
With its caves of mystery.

Cheddar Gorge is marvellous
The Mendip Hills abound,
Whilst in the moors below
Much wildlife is found.

Wander in the meadows
Trek the leafy lanes,
Pause to watch the birds
Enjoy the gentle streams.

The magic of Glastonbury
And grandeur of Wells,
Are where you must not hurry,
The saints would have us dwell.

The villages delight
With character and charm,
You cannot fail to see
An English country farm.

Taunton is the tops
As our county town,
With its many shops
Much can be found.

Try Weston or Burnham
Healthy spots to stay,
Or Minehead is great
To ease your cares away.

Coaching inns and mansions,
Lovely churches too,
Thatched cottages delight -
Somerset welcomes you.

Brian R Russ

THE ALLURING AISLES OF SAINBURY'S

(A variation on 'The Lake Isle of Innisfree' by W B Yeats)

I will arise and go now, and go to Sainsbury's,
And a large trolley trundle, of steel and plastic made;
Nine aisles there will I survey, each lined with groceries,
Piled high and all-enticingly displayed.

And I will spend the morning just dawdling to and fro,
Weighing up the value of the more exotic buys
Against the 'special offers' that in my trolley go -
The money off or chance to win a prize.

I will arise and go now for in my mind I see
The bright lights of the superstore still beckoning to me
And shoppers at the check-outs buying pizzas, beans and tea -
Some clearly labelled, 'Buy Two, Get One Free'.

Sheila Burnett

LOVE'S MAGIC

If you ever think I am not true,
Perhaps when I smile at another,
Remember always I love only you.

I know you are watching all I do,
With jealousy or pique sometimes.
If ever you think I am not true.

Think from what small seed love grew
To absorb all our world around us.
Remember always I love only you.

You know a magic binds us two,
And bewitches us both with joy.
If ever you think I am not true.

Troubles may come that you will rue,
Then my darling cling on to me.
Remember always I love only you.

Keeping our love safe in today's world,
Forsaking all others our lives long.
Remember always I love only you,
If ever you think I am not true.

Joan Chapman

THE FLOWER

Once, I could not believe
That we would part. You made me
Realise that love's tremulous fragrance
Could fade, slowly, wistfully.

I wanted to make it easier
For you. Shadows smudge my eyes,
For deep within me I grieve. For the scar
Of you will remain, like a dying flower,

Ready to blossom, but which without
Nourishment, will never be. I stare
At the flowers between my fingers, entranced,
Realising how fragile it is, how little it takes

To destroy it. I would crush it, and breathe
The last choking scent, before it withers and dies.
But I cannot. For you are the strength of my fingers,
And I am the flower. I cannot be crushed again.

Gill Watson

AUGUST MAGIC

Oh, how I love the dawn of August
after a long, hot summer night.
The faint haze which follows a frost
as autumn begins to bite.

There's a sense of change in the air
as summer begins to fade.
No other month can compare
to the delight of each new August day.

The dark blue sky starts to lighten
as night now fades away.
Then the sun starts to brighten
as the sweet dawn meets the day.

There's a beautiful hush
as nature unfolds
all plants green and lush
waking up from the cold.

The birds start to sing
their happy dawn call:
may this new day bring
hope and joy, to us all.

Rosemary A V Sygrave

THE CHURCH OF DESTINY

Cycling in Dorset, a delightful old county,
Of which England is rightfully proud,
Woodlands, now tinted on this warm autumn evening,
We, just two lovers, avoiding the crowd.

On quiet back roads, the darkness now falling,
Our destination, the sea, many miles away,
Very soon now we must stop for the night
And with no one to ask, we knew that the task
Was too urgent to make easy our plight.

It was no use pretending, we had misread the map,
Pretty villages now far behind,
With St Christopher's help, the friend of the traveller,
Not the chance of a bed would we find.

Tired and weary, in the now failed light
Was an old towered church we would enter;
We clung close together in the gloom and the silence,
Somehow afraid, but of what?
Perhaps we imagined some bright shining light
That would point us the way and lessen our plight.

We stayed there no longer, feeling cold and afraid,
But there in the porch was an old tattered map
Opened and marking a village.

We pedalled along for less than a mile,
And the folk of the cottage where we stayed the night
Insist there's no church. They just smile!

We oft drive that road on our route to the sea
And there stands the church in the bright light of day.
There is now no map, so we pray thanks for that mile
But our friends of the cottage still insist there's no church.
They just smile!

Edgar Wall

BATH ABBEY COURTYARD

Perpendicular spires
Blocking the sun,
Loom over tourists,
Whose clicking cameras
Sweep the scene.

A guitar-plucking busker
Growls out folk songs
To ignoring crowds,
Someone takes pity,
Throws him a coin.

Fat, complacent pigeons
Strut between the legs
Of elderly folk
Knowing they'll get fed
With scraps of bread.

Beneath bright flowering baskets
Drop-outs gather on steps
Hairy and grimed,
They smoke their joints
With vacant eyes.

One offers the 'Big Issue'
To smartly-dressed women
With bulging bags
From expensive shops.
They hurry on.

A harassed mother rushes by,
Her baby is screaming.
Then in the distance
The sound of a flute
Hauntingly sweet.

Gwen Hoskins

TIME TRAVEL

Phoning Australia
Just to reminisce
Of weekends even wilder
More full-on than this
From the back of a limo
To the outback in a tent
Ten digits on the mobile
Round the globe our chat went.
Here among friends though
Nothing's not allowed
A night with no sleep
You start dreaming aloud
Out of the comfort
Zones of our heads
Where truths are unearthed
And things get said.

Mark Tuck

SUMMER

Summertime we call it
Rain, rain, rain
When will the sun appear again?
I think I have a tan or is it rust?
I must get some sun
I must, I must
People say the summers were so good
I wish they could return
Oh I wish they would.

Bubbles Gaynor

WHY THE SALAMANDER?

Salamander, Salamander.
Why you, Salamander?
Your word, like a hailstone in a thunderstorm
hitting the hard surface but staying whole
and later disappearing
and then reappearing.
Imprinted boldly
on the inside of my forehead.

Salamander, Salamander.
Forging yourself in black.
A lizard like creature living in my fire.
Why not a common newt or toad
that might sleep upon my pillow.
Why not a tailed amphibian
that likes to lie on moist surfaces
and leave at dawn.

Salamander, Salamander.
Casting yourself in iron behind my eyes.
Waiting for other words.
Waiting for other words to mould you
on the page and douse my fire.
These are the words
Salamander.
These are the words.

Grace Gauld

HAYMAKING

Oh where have all the flowers gone?
The farmer's shining blade has come
And chopped their heads off - every one!

In convex rows across the field
The grasses fall, their stems revealed,
And in their pale green stalks concealed.

Limply the fallen flowers lie.
Tall campion and white ox-eye
Droop their bent heads and slowly die.

For haymaking has come again
And boys and girls run down the lane
To help the farmer fill his wain.

And by the evening all is done,
The grasses stacked, the meadow shorn -
But all my lovely flowers have gone.

Evelyn Westwood

THE ROYAL BRITISH LEGION

I'm a member of the Legion
For Queen and country and all that
Most people of my age
Think it patriotic crap

Each November 11th
I wear my poppy with pride
I stand tall at the memorial
Feelings stirring deep inside

I respect the silence
Standing still with lowered head
I'm not the religious kind
But I pray for our war dead.

I stand and I remember
Those who died without a fuss
I stand and I remember
They won freedom for each of us.

Gillian M Morphy

SADNESS

With a beam of sunlight
the trees had become silhouetted
against a blue sky,
the set-aside fields
yellow in their barrenness.
Then a cloud covered the brightness
and the countryside,
which had been for a moment so real,
reverted to itself again,
empty and still under a winter haze;
a time for contemplation,
a place where your face
became moist,
salty with the drops of tears,
crying,
crying,
crying.

D Parrott

THE BUTTERFLY

A butterfly rests
And opens its wings
It's a beautiful creature
One of nature's things.

It sits in the sunlight
Colours shining bright
Warming itself
After the long flight.

Its journey began
A long time ago
As a caterpillar
That started to grow.

The caterpillar felt ugly
So it hid away
Enshroud in a cocoon
Away from the light of day.

A few months passed
And changes had occurred
It was no longer ugly
It had wings, like a bird.

It escaped its cocoon
Which had been its home
Fluttered into the sunlight
Destination unknown.

Lisa Bennett

EVENING STAR

Evening has come: a solitary star
Winks on the world with unrefracted ray;
Now, in imagination, there you are,
As vibrant in my heart as yesterday.

When morning breaks, the star will fade away,
Like my imaginary love for you;
Then I shall ache till next I hear her say:
Evening has come. Arise! Begin anew.

S H Smith

PATHWAY TO HEAVEN

I walk these fields of life
And dreams,
Where nothing is what it appears
A lie it seems.

To search for the very truth
Of how to feel,
Unravel what is not, and that
Which is real.

Seeing through the haze of smoke screens
A woven veneer,
Uncovering the truths beneath,
All the hidden fears.

They talk about our web of destiny
Our existence holds,
As we wander the worn paths
Surprised at what unfolds.

Will I find all the answers?
As I try not to stray,
See the lights of peace and harmony
On my weary way!

Derek Pile

A TESCO TROLLEY'S LAMENT

I've been pushed, shoved around the store,
Leant on hard with kids sitting in my frame
Or kicking as we pace the shiny floor.

It's no wonder that I'm feeling lame;
Now she's stopped to have a chat
I'm getting much too old for this game.

Oh! Now someone's pushed into my back,
Off we go again. Tins of beans
Cakes, buns, sticky tarts, rolls from that high rack.

No, she never buys fruit or healthy greens;
It's fizzy drinks, coke, crisps and salted nuts
The kids' clothes are all bursting at the seams.

It's rubbish food with which she stuffs their guts,
So obese, waddling on their chunky shoes
Too lazy to cook, she takes the short cuts.

She has loaded me to the very brim,
I simply cannot carry any more
Now . . . hmm. Now for the check-out, hmm it's looking grim.

Sowe are off along the shiny floor
And out to the big car park by the stream,
She throws open the boot and each car door.

Shopping unloaded, the kids let off stream,
Now she will push me to my trolley bay
Oh no! This can't be true, say it's a dream.

It's so cruel to treat me in this way,
She's driven off and pushed me in the stream
And this is all the thanks I get today.

Dumped as if I was a load of wire
And I don't even charge a 'euro' for my hire.

Barbara Watson

CAMEOS

Life is made up of miniatures
Joy, sadness, pleasures, pain.
A cocktail of emotions
Too complex to explain.

The cry of newborn babies,
The fleeting glance of death,
The ecstasy of sweet success,
A long and lingering breath.

The energy of striving
Amid the cut and thrust;
The effort to establish faith
Relationships and trust.

The freshness of a bright spring day
A rainbow in the sky;
The mellow shades of autumn mists
As flowers fade and die.

The friendships long and lasting,
The kindnesses received.
Those long remembered failures
And cherished hopes achieved.

A kaleidoscope of images
So varied in their form;
The comfort of enfolding peace
The violence of storm.

They all make up the shades of life
In ever changing ways;
From birth to death enriching
The swiftly passing days.

Joyce Reeves Holloway

DODO

The Dodo had no enemies.
He cried but could not sing.
He tried to fly but could not rise
on useless stumps of wing.

His feathered corporation begged,
'Release my rolls of fat.'
He waddled on short yellow legs
his peaceful habitat.

No neck. A big white ball for head.
Black bill grotesquely bent.
He preened himself with care. He had
a placid temperament.

Untroubled by arithmetic
he loved one mate alone.
She laid one egg. He loved this chick.
A portly paragon.

The Dodo had no enemies.
He thought his joy would last.
About his island paradise
the seasons paused and passed.

The turtle day-dreamed on the sand.
Surf hushed. The gentle dove
crooned comfort in the palm. The land
was redolent with love.

The trusting Dodo had no guile.
He saw a boat and blinked.
Man landed on the Dodo's isle.
The Dodo is extinct.

Peter Gillott

SIGN OF THE TIMES

I have no need of you
To show me to my chosen destination;
I know the way
And I am only passing through for recreation.
But still I notice you,
I feel a certain sense of admiration
For you have resolutely stood the test of time
And still give rise to fascination.

Erected when the motor car was young,
Long before the motorways;
Journeys wound their way through villages,
Along the ancient carriageways.
Time like traffic passed you by so very slowly,
For they were peaceful days,
Between the wars, before the fabrication
Of the mass-communication maze.

Beside the country public house
You gave the refreshed traveller direction;
At the parting of the ways within the villages
You offered navigational correction;
On the corner near the farm
The family could make a choice from your selection,
In the garden by the roadside
Presenting distances with due perfection.

I look at you and see the past,
Sturdy wayside director of the journeyman,
And I would bid you tell
Tales of travellers from since your vigil first began.
Survivor of the seasons and the decades,
Finger posts arranged to compliment the journey's plan,
A once-upon-a-time benevolence
To those who made their way in lorry, car or van.

Bob White

WINNING?

As the wind blows through your hair,
The javelin is almost there,
Shame you're running the hurdles,
Now there is no time for dawdles,
Feet placed firmly in the blocks,
Shame the others have fancy socks!
3, 2, 1, Bang!
Off you ran,
Pumping as hard as you can go,
Over the hurdle, only 10 more to go,
Darting over each one,
You know you've almost won,
But what's that on the outside?
If he beats you, you won't survive,
10 metres left, it's neck and neck,
As you duck together on the line,
Now it's photo-finish time,
'Yes, yes the gold is mine,'
And the world glitters with,
A beautiful shine.

Christopher Hayward (12)

OH! TO BE FAMOUS!

Oh! To be famous! To have my name up in lights
To be able to pull in the crowds
To make people laugh, to see them have fun
To walk with my head in the clouds.

Oh! To be famous! To be able to dance
To quote Shakespeare or to play in a band
To sing like a lark, fool about like a clown
To have an audience eating out of my hand.

Well, I guess I'm a dreamer in a fantasy world
And these yearnings are never to be
But when you visit the theatre or turn on your telly
Take a good look, it might just be me!

Christina R Maggs

THE STRANGER

The hand on my shoulder, from a stranger passing by,
Showed me, they understood . . . the reason I cried.

The stranger spoke, so many words,
But from their lips . . . no sounds were heard.

This gesture simple . . . and yet so kind,
In this troubled world, is hard to find.

The tears that I shed . . .were not for me,
But for the love one . . . I could not see.

When I turned to look . . . and see, who was there?
In the face of this stranger, I saw compassion and care.

Have faith said the stranger . . . do not despair,
The lives of our loved ones are not always fair.

I gave way to my grief . . . my body ached with the sobbing
I felt gentle arms surround me, like a child I was rocking.

I closed my eyes from the world . . .that I did not want to see
Since the loss of my loved one, I had felt my grief . . . was set free.

In the chapel . . . at the Garden of Rest I had come to pray,
For my loved one . . . who with the help of a stranger . . . lay
        Now at rest!

Sylvia Connor

THE WEATHER IN THE STREETS

The garden stretches its short brick laid length,
A span not very much removed from here
Keeping its balance between far and near
Towards the further limit of a fence.

Here where the brightness of the day remains
Two students kiss close to the kitchen door.
I am remembering the days before.
Then angels sang; now earthbound music reigns.

The sky's cloud shadows darken down the trees
Fruit falls unheeded unpicked on the earth
A helicopter buckets on the breeze,
Autumn drags slowly towards winter's birth.

Everything in the garden is not lovely
Love has to choose between its tricks and treats.
Wait.
Lift your head.
Loving is still behovely,
Lovers still greet the weather in the streets.

John Brackenbury

FEELINGS FOR PETER

Each new day is passing by,
Do you still feel the same?
Or will our memories and feelings,
Fade hazily away.

You haunt my dreams at night,
Your image is so clear,
I feel I can almost touch you,
Feel you close to me.

Wonder what you may be feeling,
If our hearts could beat as one,
In truth we are now separate,
Until we meet again.

When we do my feelings will return,
Emotions too strong to hide,
I'll see the love burn in your eyes,
I'll feel the warmth rush from your heart.

Kim Brogan

MY NEXT SUMMER HOLIDAY

Next year's holiday: Where shall I go?
I've come here now six years in a row!
My parents used to come again and again
But this is now whereas that was then.

It's time for a change, I'm sure of that.
The cash I've spent could have bought this flat.
I'll just sit out in this lovely sun.
Won't get the car, though it needs a run.

Must send some cards, though they're just the same,
Sent them last year, well I'm not to blame
If they don't print new ones every year
I'll write them soon with a pint of beer.

The office gang will say 'Not again?
How many times now? It must be ten!'
Here comes the clerk with the booking form,
'Same weeks next year? I know that's your norm.'

I should have said 'No' and made a stand
But the view from here is just so grand,
I could travel further and fair much worse,
Booking's provisional, I can always reverse.

Keith Lainton

PERPETUAL MOTION

Have you seen those useless gadgets that swing or sway or bounce?
They're a very potent symbol of the lives we lead today.
We're never still.
We rush around.
Our days are crammed from dawn to dusk.

This age of new technology
Should ease our lives, we're told,
We should have time for leisure
To savour new pursuits,
Instead, we seize the chance to earn,
To take on new commitments.
We're tense and stressed,
Our tempers frayed,
We've ailments never heard of.

Please stop! Slow down!
Enjoy the simple pleasures.
Relax your body and your mind
And you'll feel so much better.
Take time to look around,
Revel in nature's beauties,
Take time to talk,
Take time to walk,
Renew neglected friendships.

The years pass all too quickly,
Then it's too late to regret
You had a senseless aim in life
To never waste a moment!

Roma Davies

YESTERDAY'S CHILD

Pennies for sweets,
　　Occasional treats,
Whips and tops,
　　And lollipops.

Clockwork toys,
　　Simple joys,
Tiger Tim,
　　Remember him?

Trips to be made
　　With bucket and spade,
To sands and sea,
　　Such bliss for me.

Came September
　　And sad surrender
Of hopes for peace,
　　So soon to cease.

Farewell to sweets
　　And special treats,
Just bread and jam,
　　Dried eggs and spam.

Sirens wailed,
　　Long nights prevailed,
Old foes returned,
　　And London burned.

These dark days passed,
　　Peace reigned at last,
Cheers ascended,
　　My childhood ended.

J M Armstead

COSY

I am comfortable in bed,
Warm from toe to head,
Reading my book by Jane Payne,
Listen to the sound of pelting rain
                  on the windowpane.

Before I turn the next page, I look up and gaze,
At the pelting rain on the windowpane,
This lack of sun leaves me dull and my head in a haze,
I enjoy my bedtime glass of wine
Listen to the pelting rain on the door of pine.

My eyes are drooping sleep hails,
Time to recharge my battery cells,
My tired eyes fall,
Until the morning call
Listen to the sound of pelting rain on the windowpane.

M Wood

WE'LL MISS YOU MEG
(For Meg, a missed horse)

You've got to understand why you're going,
We've all lost will to be strong and it's showing,
We will stay together in our heart,
Experiencing the pain of being apart,
The road is rough but you'll get through,
Moving on the starts are new,
We're all going to be missing you,
But eventually you will pull through,
We all know that it will be hard but we'll try,
I suppose this is a way of saying goodbye.

Sarah Linsdell

A GODLY SOLDIER

'And, 'What are you in for son'
'Cowardice, sir' I said.
But, I didn't really believe it
But the word ran through my head
'It astonished me so'
Said I to the jailer
'In the face of battle'
I'd found jelly for two legs,
I found I couldn't move out forward
And couldn't run away
So, in the midst of battle
I just knelt down to pray

O' they thrashed me bodily forward,
And hung me by the neck,
Scupper'ed me fore and aft
Among the lower deck

It's lucky I'm alive, sir,
I guess it's true to say
I'm the living proof of cowardice
I die a little each and every day.

O' The jailer then took pity
'Up the keys' he said,
He then struck me politely
Upon my upturned head
'Get in line,' hollered the jailer,
'Turn smartly up ahead,'
O' The jailer set me free that day
And smiling, turned away his head.

R J Collins

RIPPLES ON THE WATER

We threw pebbles on the sea
in a happy mood you and me.
Full of laughter, we did stare.
The ripples on the water disappear.

We threw stones you and me
on the river. Then we were three.
After a while, laughing, full of joy,
throwing stones with a little boy.

We threw pebbles on the sea,
in a serene mood, you and me.
Our grown-up son had left home,
we were quite content to be alone.

The years and seasons passed by
Sitting down on a warm day.
Throwing stones, landing near,
together the future we didn't fear.

On the river, throwing a single stone,
sadly saying goodbye, all alone.
Misty eye, the vision isn't clear.
The ripples on the water disappear.

Licia Johnston

AFTERWARDS

When I am gone don't mourn for me
be glad and not a tear should fall.
No flowers plant except forget-me-not
to show you will remember.

Do not grieve and do not weep,
the love in your heart give now
and show to me but do not keep,
for when I've gone it can be left unsaid.

I give to you eternal love today
for tomorrow, after I've left,
I shall know that you live on
in happiness that I have been your way.

Frank Ede

LET THERE BE PEACE

Some seeds are eaten by birds,
Others never manage to take root.
Some are destroyed as their heads poke up into winter frosts,
Others find themselves overshadowed and wither away.

Some seeds become roses,
Beautiful to behold.
But beneath the velvet petals,
Are thorns keeping you at bay.

Some seeds become daffodils,
Blowing in the wind.
But behind that sunny outlook,
Lies a future so short.

Some seeds become weeds,
Reproducing, spreading, overtaking.
But they too can be beaten back,
For their roots are shallow.

Yet some seeds become poppies,
Striking, strong and calm.
A symbol of human courage,
A reminder of those who have gone before.

People are like flowers,
Let us all be poppies.

Marie Croucher

FORBIDDEN LOVE

My love for you is so strong, even though I know it's wrong.
 I see myself in you maybe this is why I am attracted to you.
  My heart is in emotional limbo,
   but what can I do if I am in love with you.
    Heaven has sent me my guardian angel,
     my soulmate I have yearned to meet,
      but my heart aches for the lover I can never have to keep,
      but what can I do if I am in love with you.
       When we are together it's ecstasy we are so compatible,
        it feels it was meant to be,
         but you belong to another so it can never be,
         oh my lover, what have you done to me?

Bahar

OPPOSITES

You like your music classical
While country is my thing
You buy me dangly earrings
When I would have liked a ring
You take me to the cinema
When I'd really love to dance
I'd boogie down the whole night long
Given half a chance
Partying is not your style
And theatre's not your cup of tea
You're happy with a quiet night
In front of the TV
I guess that we're just different
And no one is to blame
But just for once it would be nice
If we were both the same.

Linda Hughes

MY TALE OF LOVE

We have a loving tale,
of beautiful love,
in our loving hearts,
a tale of precious love,
from our loving start.

We pleasure our hearts,
with our loving dreams,
our sweet love so true,
it comes from our dreams.

Our love came to our hearts,
with a loving caress,
then in our loving hearts,
we were heavenly blessed.

A loving tale of love,
so loving and kind,
will stay in our loving hearts,
to the end of all time.

We see a shining 'Star',
looking at our beautiful love,
the 'Angels' watched our love,
from heaven above.

We gave each other love,
with a passionate smile,
telling our loving hearts,
our sweet love will last a long while.

We are loving so truly,
and so much in love,
we thank our lovely 'God',
in his heaven of love.

Kenneth Matthews

THE DAY THE WORLD WENT MAD

Tuesday 11 September 2001, the world went mad.
It came about by people who are very bad.
Terrorists, who took their own lives
Along with thousands of others.
Lots of different nationalities
All kinds of race
Killed by people, yet without a face.
Hatred, anger and rage fills your mind
What right have they got to kill mankind?
War is not the answer
Revenge would not be sweet
Who knows what will happen
If the enemies ever meet.

People have lost friends, loved ones and colleagues
Going about their every day lives
Only to be killed
By cowards in the sky.

Our thoughts are with the families
Whose future may seem bleak
But life must go on
Around the havoc that's been reeked.

Let's hope that if there is a God
He's watching down on us
And makes the people who make the decisions
Get rid of all the bad
This world would then be
A better place to live.

Debbie Barnard

SEASON'S DAWN

The season's dawn,
As I put my hand
On the frozen windowpane,
The ice melts
And runs down,
Onto the sill,
Flowing like little rivers,
Finding their way to the sea,
Winter wind blows,
Naked trees shiver,
In the ground,
Until springtime
Comes around
Everything is new,
Fresh and growing up,
Sunshine lights up
And the rain stops,
Green fields turn golden,
Bonfires smoulder,
Echoes of children playing,
On long warm evenings,
Humid days and nights,
As the air hangs still,
Moved on by autumn's breeze,
Willow trees sway
And reach for the river,
Sending ripples to the bank,
As the cycle runs once more,
Walking up to the frozen door,
I enter another season's dawn.

A Starbuck

My Nan

I miss my nan; I loved her so,
And the love I feel will grow and grow.
She will always be in my every day living,
Always so kind and always so giving.
Not sweets or things bought from a shelf,
In my nan's life, she gave herself.
Winter, summer always there
Never biased, always fair.
That's your auntie's, don't sit there,
I didn't care, but I didn't dare.
Christmas, walking up the street
Came the patter of excited feet.
I wonder what nan's got for me.
Christmas pudding I watched her make,
Mince pies, rolls and Christmas cake.
A pair of knickers, some plasticine.
A kiss, a cuddle, a smile, my nan,
That's enough for me.

Patricia Heath

Leaving Home

Once again I am leaving
The place that is my home
This time, (a time of grieving)
I don't want to roam.

Looking round at my possessions
I really have no choice
I don't want to go
But I've lost my voice.

There are others, far too greedy
Always wanting more
Would not let me stay here
Edged me from the door.

I'll be all right, I always am
I'll make a house another home.
There will be time for grieving
This time, last time, no more to roam.

Elizabeth Morton

CONTEMPLATION

As I ponder my life past,
my brain rushes on
to contemplate life future.

The unexpected has become the norm,
life turned upside down
like an image in a pond.

Long held thoughts and notions
rocked to the foundations,
left dangling and adrift.

Certainties now wavering,
the boat adrift and moving
to a place not known by me.

The outcome is unsure
the future unclear
the contemplation continues.

Michelle Quinton-Jarvis

SHOW JUMPING AT HICKSTEAD

Seated in the stands I watched with admiration
Horse and man with so much dedication,
Even with my inexperience I could see
Man and horse in complete harmony
Beautiful creatures with grace and power
To reach such perfection must take many an hour
Horse and rider, rhythm and rhyme
For the best results they must be in time
This, my first time at Hickstead a pleasure for me
What a performance for all to see.

Gladys C'Ailceta

THOUGHTS

A garden filled with beauty fair
Brings one peace beyond compare
A garden filled with flowers seems
The epitome of all my dreams
Sweet-peas, foxgloves - roses too
Reds and yellows - shades of blue
Beauty unmatched in all its glory
Just one part of nature's story
But winter brings its savage climes
Round about the cold wind winds
Again to spring one's thoughts will fly
The beauty gone - again is nigh
And so full circle turns the wheel
Of natures sentence and repeal
So savage - yet its tender kiss
Fills ones heart with perfect bliss.

T C Hollis

ASK

I know you are hurting inside
The feelings for me you have to hide
Talking about me with your mates
Must give you a feeling inside that is just so great.

You seem shy to ask me out
Instead you tell a lie not really what it's all about
Say he fancies me that's what you've done
But feelings are stronger now it's not any fun.

Ask me out the answer may be yes
Or may be no but stop being such a pest
You're driving me insane
With you feeling you can't contain.

Let it out let it be free
To my heart you may hold the key
Be true to your feelings, they are always right
Ask me out for tomorrow night.

Ask me to dinner or a film first
If you don't ask me now, your heart will surely burst
Your feelings will come out in the end
But we could end up not lovers but friends.

So ask the answer is now sure to be yes
I know your love is one of the best
I need you now, here with me
For you're the one with the only key.

Anouska Louise Aitkenhead

ENGLAND

Once likened to a jewel, set in a silver sea,
England stood untarnished for all the world to see.
A healthy, happy land, we proudly loved to know,
Blessed with all the assets that nature can bestow.
We still have pastures rich, lush green with the rain,
And quaint little country villages with many a leafy lane.
Bluebell woods and forests, mountains, lakes and streams,
Sandy coves and beaches - the Island of our dreams!
But in any ideal garden weeds can struggle through,
To mar the adjacent beauty and spoil it for me and you.
And so it is with humans - some simply cannot abide
Conforming to decent standards, self-respect and pride.
There's an element of evil in our midst today,
Like the poisonous ivy it seeks to creep its way
Into the lives of our people, attempting to destroy
All that we're entitled and privileged to enjoy.
The seeds of hate and violence, selfishness and greed,
Need to be uprooted and not allowed to breed.
The world, of course, has changed and progress has taken its toll
Though ordinary folk, friendly and kind, remain the same on the whole.
But gone are the carefree days of spirit and of mind,
Apprehension and fear have spoilt it for mankind.
For a spiritual awakening there is a dire need,
With love and respect for each other, whatever our colour or creed.
We must strive to achieve for ourselves a united society
And enjoy again the fruits of peace and harmony.
Free and patriotic, we have a glorious past
And pride in our heritage is something that should last.
Let's set a shining example and endeavour again to be
A country to be proud of, with honour and dignity.

Constance Pugh

TUNNEL VISION

When years ago I tramped along this valley
Enchanted by a landscape so peaceful and serene,
The Channel's lapping waters stretched beyond sight,
Whilst chalky outcrops bounded a countryside unspoilt.
Through quiet lanes around arching coastline I wandered
Until I reached Shakespeare Cliff's dramatic apex.
From grassy summit I surveyed the prospect inland
Where acres of poppy-strewn golden cornfields
Sloped down in the remoteness of Farthingloe valley.

Now, today, I stand and gaze across the Channel
And glimpse a buoy almost too small for sight.
I recall faithful Edgar's account for sightless Gloster,
How fishermen who walked upon the beach below
Appeared like mice, whilst gatherers of samphire
Half-down the cliff pursued their perilous trade.
Such dizzy heights, so horribly steep, are described
From which a despairing monarch might topple headlong -
For a moment the playwright's imagining is my reality!

From remembrance of King Lear's suicidal fantasy
I return, to look upon a glistening ribbon
Of tarmac black, where earth has been gouged away
To transform the country for miles beyond Shakespeare Cliff.
The burrowing machines have achieved their purpose:
Now mainland Europe is merged in England's heritage.
And what has been gained by this tunnel vision?
Speedily we can now rush by, unseeing, where Nature's
Beauty used to reign in a landscape of peace.

Harry Higginson

A POET'S HIGHWAY

As I travel along this lone highway
    at my side my true love only,
to bring solace, joy and hope,
    an awareness of the sad and lonely
path trodden by the Son of Man,
    bearing endless rejection: sometimes,
the sickening doubt of faith and hope
    yet bless the knowledge of His bidding,
that I too must tread a lone highway
    with my true love, the true path: His way!
Disillusionment with the human race
    of grasping greed and selfishness,
precious little thought or care
    self, possessions, inward vision,
shrinks from truth; hides in falsehood and pride,
    as an instrument for Him do strive:
bid man see, learn, listen and understand
    shed his blinkers his false pride,
hopefully to seek the closure of this Day
    as I trudge knowingly 'tis a Poet's Highway!

Howard Thorn

THE BURNING BUSH

Smoky Joe resides in the White House
He doesn't believe there is global foul air
Only the wild fantasy of ecologists
Away with Kyoto and all talk of green and fair.

So shovel the coal in the furnace
The US dollar must prevail.
Speed up the generators to high pace
US capitalism must not fail.

So - let us heed well that warning
These men would drown the world
The sacred world of profit
Neath the banner of greed unfurled.

Let's build the protest movement
George Bush needs a rebellious call
Before the oceans lap around our feet
And all civilisations may finally fall.

Dave Davis

THE GIRL FROM AMSTERDAM

She looked so forlorn waiting in the Tonbridge Station booking hall,
'I have to be at Gatwick for a five o'clock flight,
How long to Redhill?' she called,
To passers-by without the time to worry nor be polite.

I felt concerned, yet why? She was only someone from Amsterdam
A foreigner - why should I care?
But I did. Someone ought to give a damn -
        show the flag a little when they can.
To give a kind of kindness nowadays seem so rare.

'It's three o'clock now, what can I do, should I get a taxi?'
I checked the price for her and somehow knew
The money involved would still leave her in a quandary.

I said, 'Why not get to Redhill, then take a cab from there?'
'Would it be under ten pounds?' she asked,
I couldn't say - I just wished I'd had more time to spare,
To drive her to Gatwick - what is more enjoyed the task.

But I was already late for work,
Trouble on the line - compelled to be somewhere,
My time was owed making a living - unable to share a perk,
Nor her to take away a memory of care.

Anthony Michael Doubler

UNTITLED

We used to joke in the war
That our little island
Would sink into the sea
Now you really wonder if it is a possibility.

The amount of troops were just passing through
Shopping in Oxford Street just around the corner
With our wonderful mother and some of gran's clothing coupons
On my day in lieu.

No matter how busy our mother was
We will never know how she did it all
Working, queuing, cooking
No one knew
But she was always there for you.

After the bombing and the noise
Oxford Street, quiet and serene
Off-the-peg clothes - pretty colours, so inexpensive
You would have to be there to see what I mean.

For just awhile it was great on such a day
Then everyone paid their way
In 'Dennis's you could buy 'Dereta'
That was when you were not thinking about Hitler.

Phyllis O'Connell (Hampson)

FAITH IN LIFE

Walk in small footsteps
Along the quiet way.

See all that you do
And hear all that you say.

Don't worry for tomorrow
Or the things of next year.

Focus all of your being
In the moment that's here.

Mary Biggs

ARE YOU WAITING?

For sun to come out from the clouds and shine again?
For someone's eyes to look at you with love, then so am I.
Are you looking for an empathy heart, a soulmate?
For the soul's freedom, away from sorrow? I am too.

If only you could follow me, to my world of dreams.
As I paint a picture of a world I long to see.
It's only a lonely fantasy, just colours on a canvas,
Telling you, you are not alone. For my heart's searching too,
Pencil in the tears, draw in a smile, to mask the pain.

We all have our secret world of sadness and fear,
Are you hoping for a life's companion, suited to your mind?
A rainbow or sunset that does not fade so soon?
Deep down inside our hearts, we are all looking for such things.

Keep your child's heart, then the harshness of the hell man has made,
Will not ruin you.
Are you looking to find a sanctuary, a heaven on earth?
Sorry my friend, it does not exist.
Pick up your paintbrush and complete with me, my picture of heaven
It is in my heart, as long as it is, you will be free.
Some day you will search no more, for God's golden light is
Waiting at the opening of a door
At the end of life's pathway.

S D Rose

MR ANT

Hello down there, little mister ant, going past my plate
You're in so much of a hurry, I wonder if you're late?
Maybe supper is waiting back at home with your mum
And two thousand brothers and that's when half can come
Have you all got names down there, can't do birthday too
You'd have a party every night, if only that was true
You really do look bushed halfway through your shift
But now you've found the sugar bowl, I bet that's quite a lift
Go on now and tell your mates about your luscious find
Bet that's really yummy stuff, for you and all your kind
Off you and get them and we'll see a great invasion soon
No! Don't want that, here's the back of my teaspoon!

James Barry

FAERIE

Ethereal beings, there in the shadow,
Seen at the corner of an eye,
Turn - there is nothing,
Was it an imagining,
Something of the mind?

Gossamer light,
Too quick for sight.

If you find joy
In the knowing.
Let them be there,
Working their magic,
For your contentment.

Pam Hammocks

MOTHERHOOD
(For my very good friend Hazel)

You spend nine months just waiting around
While your tummy gets closer and closer to the ground
As soon as your baby starts moving around
You get a hospital appointment to have an ultrasound.

That's the beginning, the very start of it all
The wonder and excitement never seems to pall
Babies are so trusting, so helpless and so small
You can dress them and feed them just like a living doll!

That wonderful feeling will always remain
No matter how many, it's always the same
You wouldn't give it up, for fortune or fame
You felt exactly the same when each one came.

You've given time and attention to every child
In the hope that they wouldn't grow up wild
Whenever they are naughty or whenever they lied
You always treated them fairly, and you always smiled.

Each one is so special, in their own way
From the moment they're born to this very day
You've watched them grow, you've watched them play
Even though they will leave you, a piece of them will stay.

It's been hard work, but mostly it's been fun
You've had 5 lovely girls and a much wanted son
You entered life's lottery and you certainly have won!
So relax now, cause there's not much more to be done.

Now you've got time to find the new you
What on earth are you going to do?
Stop wasting time, stop being so glum
Whatever you decide you'll always be mum.

Maggie Fairbrace

TRAPPED

I lay on the bed listening and thinking
Unable to feel, to smell or see
Trapped inside this body of mine
Wondering what was happening to me.

People come and go
Doctors, nurses, family and friends
I tried, how I tried to let them know
That I was still here just trapped inside.

I searched my body from head to toe
My nose had a twitch,
Surely somebody will see
It's me - I'm alive please set me free.

My listening was acute, more so than before
I could hear through the walls, the door and the floor
It's this or it's that, but they are not sure
Most tests tomorrow may confirm more.

Weeks passed - maybe more
I do not know
How long I have been unable to communicate
Stuck in this room.

My life is just passing please can I have more
I want to go back to the people I love
For there's still much to do
I'm not halfway through.

Listening in the quiet, my thoughts seemed to say
You've played your part, now go on your way
I felt a tingle, then I was free
My soul flew like a bird to eternity.

Lorna Young

VALLEY VIEW (INSPIRED BY THE WYE VALLEY)

Resplendent in autumnal hues -
shaded greens, golds, reds and browns,
the valley responds to seasonal change
by displaying her glorious crowns.
In one last colourful burst
before winter's toll takes hold
they glow iridescent in struggling sun,
announcing magnificence bright and bold.

Muted suddenly as days draw on,
the trees are slowly stripped
by wintry winds blowing sharp and chill,
forsaken - their coloured robing ripped.
They stand then as a skyline new,
silhouetted 'gainst greying skies,
wispy fronds swaying from seasoned trunks
wind whistling thro' with howling cries.
Winter, with its smouldering tones
of Nature's harshness, brutal frost
mingles with diamond glistening flakes of snow,
the valley resembles a landscape lost.

Yet surprises linger hidden 'neath the load,
nurtured, cherished from within.
Soon with increasing light and warmth
Winter's battle is lost to Spring.
Weakening sun struggles now to gain
superiority over clouded skies.
Trees re-robe with budding leaf, once more
regaining splendour for the valley prize.

Ann Voaden

FAT CATS

'Oh no, woe is me,
But how can this be?'
He begged of the vet, 'What's the matter?
My logic is beaten,
My cat has not eaten
For months now but keeps getting fatter.

I give it the best
As proved in a test,
With 8 out of 10 cats preferring.
It said on the tin
There's a good chance to win
And the cat on the advert was purring.

I can't bear to waste it,
The cat just won't taste it
So what can account for its figure?
Its food pile's unstable
Upon the bird table,
So why is my cat growing bigger?'

The cat's there now waiting,
Its hungry breath baiting,
Concealed in the branch of a tree.
The briefest of bounds
Away from the sounds
Of the birds flying in for their tea.

It's kept under wraps,
But cat food as scraps
Keeps birds fat, but shush, not a word.
For 8 out of 10
Of cats questioned, when,
Will express a preference for bird.

Ed King

SEASONAL CYCLE OF NATURE

S tirring from her winter slumbers, Mother Nature
P ronounces a mass awakening of plants and animals alike.
R esplendent in their blossoms, trees usher forth colour
                              in subtle spectrums,
I dle bulbs push through earth, eager to reach the sun
N urturing petals in the warmth. Everywhere, dormant animals rise,
G reeting the new year with vigour. Thoughts turn to
                              courtship and mating.

S ultry days herald the arrival of new offspring.
U ndeveloped broods are fed by striving parents with nature's bounty.
M ajestic trees and long grass rustling in the breeze offer rhythm;
M asses of insects harmonise with their buzzing;
E laborate birdsong, cascading from skies completes
                              the summer sound.
R itually, animals begin hoarding for less bountiful times.

A change in colour and shorter days announce the
U ndertones of the new season. Gold and russet leaves fall gently from
T rees, reluctant to let their clothes go. Flowers loose
                              seeds in the breeze to fall
U nder the soil, to sleep and wake when better days dawn.
M igrating birds settle on telephone lines, ready for journeys to
N ew, exotic lands. Time is precious. Life starts to slow,
                              calmly waiting.

W ith the year drawing to a close, the weather turns.
I cicles hang from bare branches like daggers;
                              snow covers the landscape.
N estling in a holly bush, a robin shelters from the deadly cold.
T iny tracks and trails in the white blanket betray
E scapees from Jack Frost's touch. Guile, adaptation, and bravery are
R equired. The strong will again take part in the endless cycle of life.

Paul Mynard

I Promised The Wind

Wind, wind, I hear you calling to me
Carry me far across the sea
You have come calling in your summer's coat
And lifted the leaves in the water to float.

I like you best when you don't shout and roar
But love to watch as you play on the shore
What do you whisper to each mighty falls?
As you tease them down mountains to sparkling pools.

Even the seabed knows of your tasks
Please don't wear that cold icy mask
A lift you give great birds as they soar
Then a helping hand to God, cleaning earth's vast floors.

In the remembering the love's gone before
Can you keep their secrets forever more?
If I make you a promise to care for the trees
One day will you carry me far on your breeze?

From the top of a mountain when it's my time to come
Will you hold me fast, then across the land we will run?

Susan E Roffey

Intensive Care

Suspended; between life and death
She lays inert, isolated: submerged
Deep within her silent unconsciousness.

Monitors graph the rhythmic beat of her heart
Chart the ebb and flow of her coursing blood
Quantify and drip feed, through transparent lines
The necessary vital sustenance that maintains her life.

Unfathomable; out of reach to those that keep vigil
Carefully stroking her hair, caressing her brow,
Wondering whether she will ever return . . .
Engaging again, in her once vibrant life.

Dennis Cohen

ENGLISH WEATHER

Birds are singing, bells are ringing,
Summer's here at last -
But hang on, just a minute -
Have the black clouds really passed?

Rain was pouring, wind was roaring
Only yesterday.
Is it any wonder
We tend to lose our way?

Winter, summer, autumn, spring,
Each newcomer once would bring
A fairly standard season,
And we would know the score.

But now the changes happen
With no ordered pattern
And little rhyme or reason,
So we seldom ask for more!

We have ever groused a lot
At our weather, cold or hot.
This is just a new phase
So that we may not get bored.

Therefore smile, doff your hat;
In a while you'll realise that
This is one of many ways
Our English sanity's restored.

K M Inglis-Taylor

THE JERSEY BATTLE OF FLOWERS

Well over fifty thousand flowers, some years,
   To decorate, a single float, must die;
But death to them is glorious. Shed no tears!
   If they could hear the cries, as they pass by,
And gasps of admiration, clapping hands,
   They'd know their early death was not in vain,
For dancing girls, and clowns, and marching bands
   Pay homage to the climax of their reign.
Now they are joined each year by millions more,
   Which all give life to many a new born dream,
As stars and birds and animals by the score,
   And Mickey Mouse, and engines puffing steam,
And perfect peacocks' tails, and lions and fish,
   And gentle Jersey cows and floral cars,
And snakes and dragons - almost all you wish
   To see - are joined by cymbals, drums, guitars.

But 'time past', when the judges' votes were known,
   The men and girls who rode, or walked beside
The beautiful creations - from the throne
   Where sweet Miss Battle of Flowers had sat in pride,
Down to the smallest handcart, dressed with flowers
   And pulled by children - made sure blossoms, torn,
Were hurled among spectators. Countless hours
   Of work were lost, but there the name was born -
'The Jersey Battle of Flowers'. The name remains,
   Though now, in darkness, floats bear coloured lights.
A glorious evening show has proved it gains
   In popularity, to reach the heights.

Long may the dying flowers their beauty give.
   As the hundredth Battle dawns they will forgive.

Mabel Helen Underwood

BYGONE BRIGHTON

Ah - those were the days, in the fifties
when Brighton was host to all sorts
there were tinkers and tailors and soldiers
and sailors from various ports.

When boys and girls danced at the Regent
with a glittering sphere up above
and the floor was alive with the power
of music and jiving and love.

Folk would visit Blackrock in the morning
and play in the pools by the sea -
catch winkles and shrimps by the dozen
and then take them home for their tea.

There were Tigers in Brighton, in those days
you could see them perform for a price
and after they'd mauled their opponents
we were all free to take to the ice.

And every New Year from the station
a message was heard, loud and clear,
from the steam trains all sounding their whistles
to herald the start of the year.

Though Brighton has changed through the ages
the Palace Pier still reigns supreme
where you get a grand view of the coastline
or sit in the sun and just dream.

Jonathan Bryant

A MOMENT IN GUADALAJARA

From the shoeshine stall I had a grandstand view
Of the simple street drama played out below.
She fingered the front of his shirt as he gazed
At somewhere beyond her, distant, detached.
Words were exchanged, though lost in the hectic parade
Of big city motion and sounds. She looked up,
Touched his chin, moved back and turned away frowning.
He called, dismayed, stretched out a pleading hand.
They formed a curious tableau, as if frozen
Briefly in an operatic trance. He laughed,
Came up and gave her ear a pouting kiss.
She nodded as he sauntered off along the street
And followed slowly for a while until he turned
A corner. There she stopped and like an anxious
Mother watched him go. I glanced down at my shoes,
Now gleaming with splendour, a drill sergeant's joy;
Too bright to seek change, so I gave him fifteen.
He murmured a gracias as I climbed down.
The show was over, I thought, when there she was
Strolling along in the crowd and as she passed
She tossed a smile . . . at me!

Rex Baker

THE PATH

We had walked the path together
For many a happy year
So when you left me I could only
Try to dry my tears.

Without you there was nothing
The path crossed an empty land
The carefully tilled fields I'd known
Had crumbled into sand.

But slowly though I could not see
I felt you were still near
That thoughts of things you'd say and do
Could comfort me, my dear.

And so I came to realise
As I stumbled on alone,
That you still walk the path with me
And you will see me home.

Pippa Suggett

SEAGULLS

Seagulls soaring up so high
Gleaming white across the sky,
Swooping, diving, floating by.

Seagulls in the spring will mate.
Sit on nests in patient state,
Hatching eggs, they quietly wait.

Seagulls calling loud and clear,
One by one their chicks appear,
Soon their cries for food we hear.

Seagulls' babies we espy,
Stretch their wings, attempt to fly,
Soon succeed as weeks go by.

Seagulls flying as before,
Young ones resting on the shore,
Parent birds are free once more.

Seagulls on the thermals soar,
Handsome birds you can't ignore
Splatting droppings on the floor!

Beryl R Daintree

WISTON SPRINGS

There where chalk meets Wealden clay
Bursts forth a spring through night and day
Quietly feeding the clearest pond
Where grows green duckweed frond on frond
Water boatmen skim along, suddenly stop
And then go on to escape the frog that hops
And dives down to depths of crystal hue
Where streaks the kingfisher's brilliant blue
And sticklebacks flash in silver streaks
To escape the predator's piercing beak
There in the evening's shimmering light
Dragonflies rainbow in glowing flight
And when the sun sinks into the Down
The evening sky with glory crowns
This precious place with golden light
And moorhens nod forth to quietly preen
Elderly gentlemen in stockings green.

David Tas

DON'T

Pretty stars,
Big and bright;
Shine a little light tonight,
Shield me from this awful fright,
That comes with each dark, blackened night.
Don't leave me here to cry and wail,
For if you do,
I'm sure to fail.
Help me find my way back home,
Don't leave me in the dark alone.

Lyndsey Power

FOLLOW THY GUIDE

Seek thee guidance from above
And life will fit like a glove
Follow thy guide
And there abide.

The sun always shines on the meek
Over-riding feelings weak
For those travelling the path of goodness
Brings to other folk happiness.

Go forward and be thee led
Thy gratification to spread
Bringing hope to all
Before the fall.

'Tis a pleasure to see
Lives open up with glee
As someone somewhere gladdens their life
Foiling all strife.

The giver also feels satisfaction
Goes without mention
They having accepted the guiding hand
That passes in every land.

Tho' life appears to change
And washed be thy brain
The true life is still there
For everyone to share.

Josephine Foreman

AUTUMN

Our close companion draws closer still
at this season of days spent on the edge of mysteries.

The rigorous contemplation of uncertainties
with the constancy of change uppermost.

Roots laid bare
and the revelations perceived through their structure.

Intimations like ghosts becoming more familiar in a landscape
full of spaces that allows them through.

Played out against a backdrop of colours
rioting on the edge of darkness

in a silence that suffuses this wordless beauty
with its all pervading sense of poignancy

the kindred spirit of this haunting ritual
of taking leave.

Judith Garrett

THE BLARNEY STONE

High up on the Castle wall
I kissed the Blarney stone.
Lying recumbent on my back,
The awkward deed was done.

Supported by the local guide
Who firmly held my arm,
I stoutly clutched the iron bars,
So not to suffer harm.

My wife was next to take her chance,
Repeating all the moves.
In order to obtain success,
The gift of Blarney proves.

And now we have certificates
For all the world to heed,
Although my wife insists that there,
In my case, was no need . . .

Leonard T Coleman

THE POWER OF THE INVISIBLE

The mysteries of life are invisible
They are silent and intangible
And as we sit in quiet prayer
Our peaceful thoughts fill the air
And in the silence of our mind
The mysteries of life slowly unwind
The spring flowers emerge from the ground
And there is not a whisper of sound
Nature's clock tells them when to rise
To wake up and give us all a lovely surprise
Spring is here again the flowers are saying
The snowdrops, their pure white gowns displaying
Quietly the sun rises each day
And time passes dreamily on its way
Softly and gently falls the night
The stars come out shining bright
And when we reach our journey's end
God will take us gently by the hand
And as the butterfly escapes from its chrysalis
Silently we will fly to the land of bliss

Sylvia Gwilt

KNOWLEDGE AND WISDOM

Is time a period or a moment?
Is it just a means of measurement?
How can you measure eternity
Where time relates to infinity?
Is gravity a property of space,
Or does matter possess a case?
Space-time involves the fourth dimension;
They are combined is the pretension.
Questions about space and time
Lead to questions about design.
Is our world the result of evolution?
Such a theory is not the solution.
Out of chaos there came precision;
Is it possible without decision?
Mathematics is a powerful tool,
And science is a precious jewel.
But neither can calculate what is right;
It needs the 'eye of the heart' for insight.
It's written, 'We reap as we sow,'
For so many actions end in woe.
There is puzzlement about the meaning of 'good';
No other concept has been so misunderstood.
Such puzzlement is queer to those who know,
The doctrine of objective value is the TAO.

Maurice Webb

IN NEW PARK ROAD, CHICHESTER

Stand by your gate and view them
Green giants in June and July
Horse chestnuts in line by the roadside
Their hugeness filling the sky.

Great limbs like the arms of heroes
Great trunks standing sentinel true,
But the traffic goes roaring past them
Without a glance at the view.

Michael Rowson

SEPTEMBER MORNING '39

The child wended her way
Across the chalk cliffs of
Dover. The sky was a
Vivid blue, the sun shone
Hot on her back.

Suddenly a single plane
Flew overhead.
The air was rent with a
Terrible sound.

He strode across the grass,
Clad in khaki,
Anxiety made his voice
Abrupt.

'Come quickly, you should
Not be on the cliffs.'
Perplexed the child enquired.
'We are at war,' he said.

'What is *war*, Daddy?'
Evacuated, she found out,
War clouded her young life.
They never lived as a family
Again.

Hilary Moore

LOUISE OF CORNWALL

'Look into my eyes,' she said.

Her words haunted me,
Down through the centuries.
I remember her eyes that were opened wide
Before me,
As she looked into my soul,
Dear Louise.

She had a face,
Strange, like a pixie.
There was a touch,
A look, a glimpse
Of the gypsy.

She had a strange way of moving,
As she swooshed in her dress rhythmically,
And looked impish, positively pretty.
Her brown hair fell down her cheeks
And she blushed a little -
A perfect figure graced her movements
As her eyes glimmered and sparkled,
And she looked away,
At the bar of the water,
In her coloured skirt,
That contained little, tiny mirrors,
That had been woven into material,
That glittered her studded dress, picturesque.

The yellow roses of Saint Endelion
Peep through the window,
In the morning of the new day.
A yellow ray
Illuminates her hair
And the vein of the stem of the flower
That blows and grows over her grave
Reminds me of her stare,
And symbolises her beauty.

The water laps like a ghost
There is a sound, 'Hello . . .'
And she looks around,
And I look up at her, into her eyes
And she says, in a whisper . . .
'Thank you . . . David.'

David de Pinna

ON RECEIPT OF A 50TH BIRTHDAY CARD

Thank you so much for your card and rhyme,
A really lovely, kind thought,
Though it's all too clear these days that I'm
Over the hill, and quite past my prime . . .
Good friendship enhances the passing of time
And helps one not to get fraught,
But to grow old with grace as one ought!

Sue Morley

LONE WOLF

Silent, angry, watchful, looking down from the hills,
viewing the rest of the wolf pack, with its many ills.
Alcoholic wife beaters, people who pass the needy by,
sad, sick people, who think feelings, are pie in the sky.
The lone wolf sees them all, dislikes them intensely,
in eating them, he would take pleasure, immensely.
But his caring mind tells him, they need help, not killing,
a few short, sharp lessons in life, if only they were willing.
If only the leaders of the pack, had shown more care,
given their cubs lessons in life, made them more aware.
Instead of ignorantly raising them, to have no heart,
perhaps the lone wolf, wouldn't feel so apart.
The world isn't changing much but the lone wolf is,
he's still a wolf, he'll probably always be a wolf,
sometimes he's a sad wolf, but not usually a bad wolf.

Danny Coleman

A GOOD CIGAR

Rapturous is the wonderment it brings by far -
The enchantment of a blissful Havana cigar,
There on a Caribbean sun-drenched isle,
Hand-rolled, the spell is cast awhile.
When Corona is lighted there comes repose,
On what contentment its flavour bestows,
These are the joys you can embrace
Through the nose and the faculty of taste.
Havana aroma has weaved its spell -
Such pleasurable contemplation no words can tell.
   A woman is only a woman, Kipling wrote,
   But a good cigar is a smoke.

Derek Marshall

LIFE OF GLASS

After four Septembers' came the day
To place a shining cube on virgin ground -
A mounting block to a donkey on the sands.
The crystal form
Reflected the primary colours of infant toys,
Shaping a wall around this single stand.
At a distance, the world revolved in crowds
In smoke-filled buses to the promenade.
Voices whispered in another room
Yet had no part to play.

The delicate charade
Left time to balance in the trees,
Lowering fragile bricks
Through tangle of convolvulus.
Catching a butterfly in the prism,
Splitting it into a blaze of orange wings.

Design became more complex with the years.
Stiff fingers urged some order,
To space the bright and clear
Between the clouded squares
That blurred like snow-packed paperweights.
Entered the annexes of man and child
Ambition formed a maze of sunlit turrets.
Dark shadows fell upon the glass
Changing the stronghold to a hollow shell,
Only to be rebuilt.

Sometimes it rained; the rain passed down the years,
Washing the brittle structure;
Each cube became a mirror
Evoking an image of the past.

Veronica Charlwood Ross

PRETENDING

I know we quarrelled a lot, but it was just one of those things,
That the state of matrimony to its participants brings.

From morning to night it went on and on, absolutely sickening,
Until it probably reached the stage when we never stopped bickering.

Then you ran off with someone else and our relationship seemed ended,
But I hoped that you'd return to talk it through, so it could be mended.

For it's not that I'm pretending I love you, it's the way I feel -
Though friends laugh, call me a fool for being faithful to an ideal,

Declaring it's time I came to my senses and accepted your flight,
That I'm well rid of you, of my single condition I should make light.

That I must forget the past, enjoy the present, now you are gone,
Claim it was better sooner than later to find you'd done me wrong -

I simply can't get over the rejection, why my love you did spurn,
When you always knew I would be waiting, pretending you will return.

Laura Edwards

THE GULLS FROM THE SEA

When winter skies are grey all day
And showers of rain sweep over the bay
When waves crash upon the shingled shore
And cliff top flowers, bloom no more.
    The gulls fly in from the sea.

Do they remember summer days
When on warm thermals they were raised
High above the dreaming Downs
And busy, friendly seaside towns.

Now it is a colder scene
With fields ploughed to a purple sheen
The gulls circle far and wide
Seeking food not brought by tides.

Their raucous cries fill the air
They have no time to pause and stare
With wings outstretched, grey barred or white
They hurry before the coming night.
        When the gulls return to the sea.

Meryl Champion

THE CLOSED DOOR

If I stopped talking
would you hear my silence?
If I was invisible,
a forgettable number
that drifts upon the pages
of life's apathy
would you even notice?
If I gave up the power
of speech
and chose the written word,
would your conscience
be the slightest bit stirred?

For here within the awkwardness
of a pause
and amongst the empty hours
that chills the stillness
before the dawn,
this is where you'll
find humanity.

Michael Wilson

FREEDOM

I look up at the spread dark night,
With its silver shimmering points of light,
Where the starry prisoners of the sky
Bejewel the couch on which they lie.

Each star rides its allotted place,
Telling the hours, marking space,
Held in an oft repeated dream,
Imprisoned forever, it would seem.

But I am not bound - by night or day.
I'm free to wander the Milky Way.
Free to live and love with thee -
For Darling - your love has set me free.

G Poole

A FAMILY PORTRAIT

As statues caught, life stilled and framed
Their faces masqued, all white unnamed.
They all were living once you know!
They all went with the ebb and flow
All frozen now with ghostly stares
Our smiles shall be the same as theirs
When from an attic's dusty nooks
Among the bric-a-brac and books
A photograph, a family group
A posed, assembled little troop
Of nephew, uncle, aunt and niece
Shall hang above the mantelpiece.

Les D Pearce

DREAM WHAT YOU WILL

Dream what you will
When you will
Where you will
And how.

Not this year
Not next year
Not sometime never
But now.

Harness your dreams to sunlight
Scenting the fragrance with dew:
Flora and fauna and near reality
Will all come true - for you!

For me -
There is moonlight over the sea
Dancing whispers of love:
Drawing my dreams to the water's edge,
Teasing my feet to move.

Forward beyond the ebb and flow
Touching the wind-drift as I go
Now breasting the waves
Now sinking below . . .
I carry all I need to know -
In my sack of dreams.

And the when and the where
And the how and the why
Are lulled in an ocean's lullaby -
Where reality is a distant sigh
And contentment is a soulful cry
Of wonder -
In my dreams.

Rosemary Watts

AWARENESS

Days are numbered from our birth,
Make each one the very best,
Some are sad, some full of mirth,
Try to fulfil God's behest.

Helping, caring, loving all,
Look around for those in need,
They will then know that their call
Is heard, you're their friend indeed.

At the break of each new day
Never fail to give you aid,
Spare some time to dear God, say,
'Thank you for the world you've made.'

No more evil, no more wars,
We could then all live in peace,
Open heart, open your doors,
Then hate and all ills would cease.

One big family, we'd be,
Love and light, surrounding all,
There's so much for you and me,
When we listen to God's call.

Suzanne Joy Golding

UNBURIED TREASURE

I watched her as she sloped across the floor,
Dejectedly, towards the garden door.
No prospect of a meal or woodland walk,
The master's locked in work and human talk.
Tail tightly tucked between her legs, ears flat,
Nothing to chase, no bird or next door cat.
Gloom in canine guise!

She sniffed her way round paths she knew so well
In search of an old, or fresh, intriguing smell,
When suddenly she stopped, with ears up straight,
With wagging tail and new spring in her gait,
She ran to where the shrubs were overgrown
And there, beneath, lay yesterday's large bone!
Bliss for several hours!

Bee Kenchington

GUARDIAN ANGEL
(For my dearest friend Pat)

You bring me a power,
Unknown to nature.
You are blessed,
With the gift of a beautiful soul.
A loving support,
You give me strength.
A guardian angel,
You will always be to me.
I love you more,
Than words can say.
You are the strength,
Within me.
You are the arms,
That hold me.
You are the heart,
That loves me.
You are the rock,
That keeps me strong.
You are the light,
At the end of the tunnel.
Always know
That I love you!

Jennifer Hayes

BUS STOP

Dancing shoes, heads straining away,
People in line to start the day.
Reluctant heads viewing all around,
No two sets of eyes meeting are ever found.
A nervous time standing still for the bus,
Evading strangers easier in the rush.
Here comes a bus, hope it's mine!
Looking at the watch but already knowing the time.
It's the one and a feeling of ease,
Hope it's empty and can sit where I please.
But the bus is half full and only seats next to others,
Looking at the choice, old men, women, some mothers.
Picking the frailest, much safer there,
Someone who won't talk or want to share.
An uncomfortable ride on the edge of the seat,
A nervous adjustment of clothes to keep oneself neat.
Bus stops count by and the journey ends,
Rush off the bus leaving others friends.

Pete Simmons

AUGUST

August will be a busy month,
With children home from school,
Variable weather, is usually the rule,
With some days hot and sunny,
Sometimes a week of rain,
Shopping to get winter clothes,
For children going to school again.

E M Apps

SUMMER SCENE

In the weltering heat
on a wheat field summer day
a boy and a mouse
caught akin in the sun's affirming rays
in the skin of the moment
at the crossing of their ways
bright eyes gleaming from the harvest mouse head
projecting multicolour joy
onto the young boy's mind
now and for future memories
repeating the feeling, the wonder, the awe
as two distant worlds in a space briefly met
as the little mouse swayed
on the ear of wheat
sharp eyes shining from its tiny head
the boy enraptured, captured by the scene
as if in a summer's dream

Pete Bauer

WATER

Dewdrops that sparkle like stars in the night,
Mountainous waves that froth, thunder and white,
Waterfalls descending, falling along
Cool trickling streams humming a song.
Wide open lakes surrounded by trees,
Gentle falling rain refreshing the leas.
Crystals falling, small pieces of moon
That glisten, then disappear quite soon.

Pamela Jennings

THE FREEDOM OF RELEASE

I am the bird that's learned to fly,
cutting a swathe across the sky.
I am the leaf that's left the bough
drifting earthward, falling now.
I am the wave that breaks on shore,
the ebb and flow for evermore.
I am the blind man given sight,
all his days no longer night.
I am the dumb man without word,
suddenly his speech is heard.
I am the deaf man who can hear
the sweetest music in his ear.
I am the beggar without worth
whose meekness will inherit earth.
I am the patient bound to die,
no longer forced to live a lie.
I am the prayer that's reached His ear
He will save those whom I hold dear.
I am the prisoner now set free,
no longer shackled - I am *me*.

Angela R Davies

GOLDEN JUBILEE - PRIDE IN A NATION

Proclaiming her popularity,
Our Queen, a symbol of love,
Superior being of infinite majesty,
Carries the sensitivity, of the sacred dove.

Her natural ability, consoling bereaved souls,
Breathing a sense of stability, gently unfolds.
Generating knowledge, of hope and faith,
A paragon of virtue, a following of grace.

Her smiling warmth cast sunlight,
Amongst the thronging crowds,
Their response is blessed from heaven,
Without even a whispering cloud.

Thank you Ma'am for all your kind deeds,
Reassuring support in our country,
Historical value will proceed . . .

Lorna Tippett

CHERISH

The murmur of your kiss
upon my lips
awakens lost desires.

The trust in your eyes
remind me of the faith
I should have had
but denied.

The scents of your body
in their most subtle forms
arise needs hidden by
damage of long, long ago.

The memory of your arms
about my shoulders
dissolve my fear of being.

Whilst you were here
- you were here but
now you have gone
- you are gone.

Michael Alan Fenton

ODE TO WILD PARSLEY

The roadsides in the country
Are decked in white array
So delicate their blossoms
They decorate the way

It seems like a church pathway
After a wedding show
With flowers like fairy lace
The height of our elbow

Every year we see this
A vision to enjoy
Some will say 'It's only weeds'
That name is a decoy

Walking in this white alley
May bring trouble to some
With runny noses and sneezes
But the scene is welcome

How does God make such beauty
So intricate its form
The whites and greens its colours
Nothing will quite conform

The ferny leaves so tender
Enhance the blossoms white
Like tiny umbrellas
In the sunshine so bright

These little sprays of magic
Adorn lots of hedgerows
Seen in tiers of beauty
Each year this picture grows

Edith Buckeridge

HARVEST MORNING

There's enchantment in my garden,
Before the world intrudes,
When air and sights and sounds are pure,
In blissful solitude.

So still, not a leaf stirs,
Only the whisper of a wakening breeze,
The plaintive cry of a distant lamb
And the hum from early bees.

Slanting sunlight crosses through the branches,
Lays pools of gold upon the lawn,
A sparkling cobweb, woven in the still of night,
Hangs on the rose bush,
With dewdrop jewels, that will not last, to evening light.

The birds have ceased their morning chorus,
Now they're diligently feeding their brood.
Flying high, silently, to their secret places,
With morsels of fledgling food.

The scent of hay drifts over the hedgerows,
That threshing machine, now stands its ground,
The scene of yesterday's toil,
With noise, dust and oil!

We now have time to gather in, make haystacks, or go bailing,
Freshly rested - we are.
A few pints of 'Old Rosy' did the trick,
Carried us home!

Clive A Baldwin

LOVED AND LOST

Out there somewhere a star shines bright
Proving to me that there once was life
A life that was dear and precious to me
That now leaves my arms so empty.

My arms long to hold a newborn life
The ache in my heart, it cuts like a knife
Babes all around me, but none are my own
Why couldn't fate have left me alone?

What have I done, where have I erred
Why have these tragedies in my life occurred
Will I ever contribute to the human race
And fill this cold and desperate space?

It's sad I know and it's making me blue
How life has treated me so cruel
Five lives tragically taken away
Leaving me fighting, to face each new day.

Every goodbye hurts just the same
I knew each one, if only by name
Tears on my pillow, each fibre sodden
For my dear babies, never forgotten.

Kate Sorby

WORDS

If there is something to be written
a word to be put in place
think carefully how one writes it
let not a memory erase.

For words are memories forever
once written their place is set,
thoughts from the mind may fade
the laid down word one never forgets.

Geoff Hume

TO THE CHILD IN ME

Do not waste your season below the dream
    level, here with me
While the sky breaks out in swallows
    and the night hawk wearily
Slips through their wings down the moon's
    cold shoulder after long vigil
Over the hosts dimly groping through a
    dumb cliff's smoke-ousted skull.

Go where the ice swims free down far off
    meadows and skilfully
Parries their sun's quick thirst,
    and inhales wilfully
Childlike, strews him, king's ransom of colours
    that fill the heart's silence
With song and fashions that fly with the
    swallows, and dance . . . and dance . . .

Never let snare trace that blessed good
    fortune's serenity
With indelible networks. Such graces are sent to be
    beauty's adornment; not hair splitting hackneyed
Truth trimmed with lies,
    but the smile that closes tired eyes when
The last swallow flies.

Norah Green

CIRCADIAN RHYTHM

Silk banners of dawn
That herald the rising sun
Colour the still air.

Resting by the lake
Trees naked and beautiful
Watch their reflections.

Rivers flow gently
Forgetting the mighty falls
That brought them to life.

Riding the thermals
Until the earth cools again
Birds float high like kites.

On the horizon
I can see a speck of blood
The sun is dying.

Crimson blood flowing
Now darkens the evening sky
Night rules the heavens.

Stars sing and twinkle
Like a thousand chandeliers
Shaken by moonquakes.

Across the night sky
The sickle moon cuts a swathe
But still the stars shine.

Silk banners of dawn
That herald the rising sun
Cut short the long night.

Jeanne Walker

THINK VERY CAREFULLY

A passport to happiness, is to stay in by yourself,
Keep away from emotions, devoid of true love.
To fly through the sky, in the emotions of yourself -
You only have yourself to please,
When the past caused your death.

When passport to happiness, finds a way into your heart
Think very carefully . . . for life's about to start
Do you want to keep away, from the treasures of true love
Keep yourself to yourself, away from emotions of the heart
Or will you find the beauty - of a once again trial?

The beauty of Earth's creatures, the child of true man
Will find you a companion, to share your happiness
Independence is a truth, when two people want the same
But the passport to happiness will be heaven inside -
Your heart will feel lighter, with arms around you outside.

You will sense strength inside, you will smile each morning
You will know someone is by your side, even if only companion
Each of us make mistakes and the past can be put to death
For is it not known, that love heals all men?
With a love so deep inside, the passport will remain.

The Passport of Happiness, is to respect your fellow man
To listen and to understand where others failed for them
To laugh and to giggle and to have a joy even in pain
To enjoy another's hobbies and not to degrade them
To look in their eyes and say, I'm glad you are my friend . . .
    Perhaps now you will understand . . .
    That another's loss is another's gain.

Josie Lawson

I CAN'T SLEEP

It's 5 o'clock in the morning
and I can't sleep.
My eyes full of heavy sting,
but I'm too tired to weep.

I've been awake all through the night,
just laying in my bed.
From when I turned out the light,
thoughts have filled my head.

I hear the breeze turn into wind,
as it rustles through the trees.
Whistling with an easy ring,
but powerful, wild and free.

The rain is fast and strong,
ticking at my windowpane.
Like a rhythmic soothing song,
the water calls my name.

The sounds of cars drive past,
and I wonder why they're out.
Making the night-time longer last,
lengthening their homeward route.

Morning is almost here,
the darkness has nearly fled.
I won't sleep now I fear,
for the night has quickly ended.

Deborah Carol Hughes

HIVE

It's daybreak and the bees have left,
The bees are on the wing,
They buzz within my head,
And creep upon my skin.

Dawn's chorus echoes all around,
And no one knows what went before,
Which is sacred ground,
Or what my bees once saw.

For all must obey the rules of life,
As the busy insects swarm,
Some sleep on oblivious,
Some wake up reborn.

Nature lays down certain rules,
And all must play her game,
Some restless in their hunger,
Others writhing within their pain.

Each has their own task,
And all are not the same,
Prey born in innocence,
Hunters bereft of blame.

As twilight falls,
Some trembling souls survive,
Within a humming harmony,
Our bees swarm to their hives.

Jim Wilson

A Thatched Cottage In Selsey

There it stood looking like a picture postcard,
Standing there looking at the beautiful cottage wasn't hard.

Flowers everywhere you look,
My breath away it took.

The rooms all looked inviting from the outside,
From one end of the cottage to the other it was so wide.

I wished I had my camera with me,
For the beauty of the cottage I would always be able to see.

The sea air was all around,
In your mind you could almost see a dog at the back of the
                              cottage bound.

Two birds were sitting on the roof, not real birds, they were
                              made from thatch,
If a cat was on the roof these birds it would not be able to catch.

Yes it really was a lovely cottage, the cottage in Selsey,
To look at it just filled my heart with glee.

Karen Grover

The Cat In Autumn

The leaves that fluttered gladly
Like flags in the summer breeze
Arc adrift and whirling madly
Round autumn's storm-tossed trees.

The cat has a climbing bout,
He mounts by hugging the ash.
From the fork his eyes stare out,
Green chinks in the ochre wash -

Reminders of summer gone
When emerald flags were flying,
That autumn must lose his throne,
Spring ascend at winter's dying.

For kittens and babes-in-arms
All is pace and change and growing;
There are no magic charms
Against time and the seasons' flowing.

S R Hawk'sbee

A VILLANELLE

Time moves on apace,
There's nothing you can do,
Accept it with good grace.

It's rather like a race,
Of course, there's nothing new,
Time moves on apace.

It's mirrored in your face,
As if this were your due,
Accept it with good grace.

For you cannot replace,
What years will take from you,
Time moves on apace.

Past feelings leave no trace,
Ideas are lost from view,
Accept it with good grace.

So now there's just a space,
Where bold ambition grew,
Times moves on apace,
Accept it with good grace.

Frances Burrow

TEA WITH AUNT LAURA

The heavy iron kettle on the black leaded grate
Spits and hisses through chalk lined lips - impatient to pour.
The big blue teapot sits warming ready.
On the mantel shelf a Jap-lac tea caddy,
With haughty Mikado kimonoed in gold scowling down at the table,
Contains best blend of Souchong and Payne's Red Label.
'One for each person and one for the pot!'
Wags the pendulum clock on the wall,
Then suddenly coughs and starts and strikes the hour.

Apple dumpling armed by the larder, bustles Aunt Laura,
Wrapped in a gingham pinafore and her own cosy aura,
Mixture of lavender, beeswax and Hudson's soap powder.
Taking a taper, she lights the lamp on the tall oak dresser
And closes the curtains at the casement window.
The room softly mellows with an oil-rich smell,
Diffusing and diminishing into an image in a crystal ball.

With the doorbell's pressing call, Laura sheds her pinafore
She pitter-patters through the hall, revealing black bombazine so neat,
To greet the widower from across the street.

Catherine Curtis

SPRINGTIME

Spring has come and all around
New life springs up from the ground
Daffodils growing in the cold earth
Once more there is new birth

Crocuses like the colour of the rainbow glow
They brighten up our day
To remind us that summer is on its way
When we gaze at this beauty what do we see -

Each flower has a purpose, you see,
Food for the butterflies and honey for the bee
Each flower adds colour to our day
Giving without seeking any praise.

A miracle that's what it must be
Given by the Lord for you and me,
Give thanks when we pray,
Flowers brighten our lives in so many ways.

Rhona Cooper

HEIR OF HOPE AND GLORY

My soul to contemplate, my mind to meditate.
A manchild born to propagate, that's why I am here;
To work to bear, my life to share: family first
Then elsewhere; surely life has more to offer
Than gathering wealth to leave another.

I know parental authority, national rule of king
And country; then heavenly law of divinity.
The carnal command of Mosaic law was given to
Those who broke the law; trespassers or
Transgressors, ignorant or wilfully
Defiling the soul unlawfully.

Hearing or reading scripture divine,
The word of truth in Christ sublime;
To turn from sin His salvation claim,
Faith in believing pardon to gain.
Gift of God, His Son, His Holy Spirit:
Eternal life I shall inherit.

Cyril Skeet

SKYSCRAPERS DIE IN FLAMES

Day by day there's news of war
Our ordered life is under threat
Many have died in dreadful pain
Lost in a fight empowered by hate.

Stress is part of modern living
Young and older we feel the pressure.
How can we bear to hear grim news?
Trivial seem our private worries.

Too soon the good times have gone by.
Did we appreciate them when we could?
Now heavy skies and thoughts are sombre,
With gloomy prospects for tomorrow.

Life goes on, as it always has,
There's work to do and mouths to feed.
Can we soothe our sorrows with music,
Or seek escape in woods and fields?

In different churches prayers for peace,
As we ask for comfort and guidance.
Will people link hands in harmony,
A sign of good will to all one day?

We must cheer up and keep hoping.
How else can we face life, be brave?
Our friends need us and we'll be there,
To keep smiling through, come what may.

Sheila Rowland

AVOIDING THE LIGHT

Darkness surrounds me
Dampness chills me
I shiver to maintain some heat
Serenely it shrouds me
No sound to disturb me
Alone, in the night with my thoughts

Soulmates are close now
Braving their duties
No glow from the cloud hidden moon
We listen for movement
No sound in the darkness
For even the enemy sleep

A flash! In the darkness
A crack! In the silence
Serenity ruptured by light
The glow of a tracer
The yell of a gunshot!
Our cocoon of darkness destroyed

The barrage of flares
That desecrates our womb
Only the strongest survive
We return to darkness
From whence we evolved
Shying away from the light.

Derek Blackburn

THE MOUNT

When the waves are parted
And the umbilical is revealed
That links, and is its granite lifeline to the mainland shore,
Meander over uneven cobbled stones
And slowly ascend where pilgrims once led the way;
Attaining the summit
Where looking back to 'quilted' fields and population's sprawl,
History's pages unfold to reveal an altogether different view:
An embattled island stronghold
With turnabout fortunes for defender and foe.
And not only to the landward side
But also from the sea,
Where English hearts were first inflamed
With sightings of the Spanish threat,
And St Michael's beacon rallied all to ensure
The challenge was - this time - well met.
Yet modern-day assailants come well-armed
Only with desire to view its past,
When stranded by the tide's swift ebb,
The moat recedes, that is its own Achilles heel
But also its abiding strength.

J Eastaugh

THE MEANING OF LIFE

We enter life in a burst of pain
But bring with us such joy
That life will never be the same
But we are but its toy.

We wonder the meaning of life
Worrying we are not enough
Should we be keeping out of strife
Or doing a lot more stuff?

Should we be finding love
Or working to cure disease
Trying to release the white dove
Or trying to abolish sleaze?

But what does it matter
When we are all going to die
All our dreams and hopes shatter
But shouldn't we still try?

Lindsey Brown

SUMMER IS GLORIOUS

Summer shines like sunbeams,
Glinting gloriously.
Summer has a heart of gold;
A face of smiling serenity,
Eyes that sparkle like the sea.
And arms that enfold it,
With constant delight.
Summer beauty is a precious sight.

Summer is like our younger days,
Full of energy and zeal.
The untiring sun blazes like a fire,.
So that people constantly perspire.
Summer daylight lasts longer;
Darkness gradually appearing,
Like a magician's trick.

Summer is like an enchanting dream,
That does not last forever.
It fades slowly away,
Like withering flowers,
But I remember its happy hours.

Linda Webster

TRULY FREE

You cannot know freedom unless you have been shackled
Where irons and torture are part of the usual tackle.
Freedom comes not from the mind but from a heart that's truly free
A heart that frees the mind at length with the beauty of a silver key.

Liberty we think we know its way
But liberty of the heart keeps imprisoned thoughts at bay.
Emancipation, release, a truly holy sanction
Yes, freedom, liberty, real emancipation.

It's a skilful heart that sets you free
Full of understanding and wisdom, ready to plea,
Unafraid to challenge, strong and bold
For on its freedom it's taken hold.

Denise Shaw

MY LOVE FOR YOU

When you hold me within your arms
Your eyes shine with all your charms
Your skin is soft and sweet
When you kiss me it feels like I've received a treat

My heart beats faster when you are near
The moment you are far away my eyes begin to fill
                    with everlasting tears

My love for you is true
I hope I will never break your heart
And hope your days will never be blue
I'll always be so in love with you.

Annette Harold

SNOWFALL

Last night it snowed and this clear morning sees a glorious shining.

White mantled hills rise smooth from unspoilt fields,
Their rutted tracks and stony hollows blank with snow,
And skeleton branches flirt their feathery flowers
On frost-nipped hedgerows, sharpened spears of grass,
While birds' thin pipings chip the shivering haze
And giddy scratches point a mouse surprised
To hungry skitterings by this shawl of snow
Where all the ugliness of corrugated rust,
Of crumbling barns, barbed wire, broken gates,
Discarded implements and plastic sacks
Is wrapped away, soft swathed in dazzling white,
Because snow fell last night and made this landscape beautiful.

But, in the deep drift below the boundary wall
A dead ewe, pregnant with lambs that will not feel the spring.

G Howarth

IN CARE

She sits in the chair,
her chair, set between *their* chairs,
her back to the window, facing inwards,
sipping her afternoon tea,
unaware of the past,
her past, packed away out of sight,
out of reach in life's locker,
of interest to no one now,
not even her.

Alan Millard

THE NEIGHBOUR'S CAT

Stealthily she treads the footpath,
Her ears alert to every sound.
I, silently, open the door,
And in a flash she turns her head,
Like a predator, she's ready to pounce.
Her eyes dare me to make a move,
I take a few steps towards her,
But she, defiantly, stands her ground.
Quickening my step, I move closer.
Then, suddenly, her courage fails,
And she turns to scamper away,
Without giving a backward glance,
And in a moment she is gone.
Now that the danger has passed,
The birds return to search for worms.
High in the trees the sentries watch,
Ready to give the warning call,
When the feline monster returns.
From my window, I can see her,
As she sneaks along the footpath,
And disappears behind the shrubs.
Overhead, the birds' warning cry comes too late!
And, triumphantly, she emerges,
Her prey clenched between her teeth.
She carries her prize past my door,
A triumphant look on her face,
As she quickly makes her retreat,
To carry her victim back home!

Doreen M Bowers

CRAB APPLES

The crab apple tree is full of fruit.
Almost overnight
The apples have burst through the canopy of leaves,
Small and green.
It doesn't seem so long ago that the tree was bare,
Brittle boughs stark against the sky,
Then tiny shoots began to decorate the branches,
And the flash of miniature blossoms could be seen
Appearing like white stars
Before the rough spring winds blew them far and high,
Perhaps before the frantic bees
Could sip their nectar and spread the dusty pollen
From flower to flower
And awaken the slumbering seed.

Yet here they are, and the tree
Is heavy with a burgeoning harvest
That swells and ripens with gathering speed
So that soon the fruit will glow like bright red jewels
Before they begin to tumble to the grass below.
The birds will perch on the laden branches
And pierce the shiny fruit, pecking out the softening flesh
With practised ease. Some will be left to grow
And maybe I will pick them, and turn them
Into glistening blush-red jelly to keep in store,
Or maybe not. Soon the crop will be over,
The leaves will fall, it will be the end of Nature's cycle,
And the crab apples will once again
Be just a memory.

Anita E Dye

SUMMER POSTCARDS

My darling Bob, wish you were here.
The roses are in bloom. I love the summer,
morning light, the promise of another day.
I hope your work is going well.
I miss you more than I can ever say.
Soon we'll be together, all love always, Sue.

Dear Mum and Dad, what weather. June's
a lovely time. Fancy, we've been married now
almost a year. We're out in deckchairs.
On the pier there's candyfloss, fat ladies, Punch
and Judy, just like all those years ago.
Hope you two are fighting fit, much love, Sue.

Dear Sis, August, noon, high noon, too hot.
The Spanish sun is beating down, unbearable.
I've put on pounds. We should have stayed at home.
Jane and John are two spoilt kids. Nothing's right.
Bob can't wait until he's back at work. Soon
the summer will be gone. Wish you were here, love Sue.

Dear Bob, it's such a lovely afternoon. I missed
July, your birthday. Sorry. Time moves on.
Your turn to take the kids away. The cutlery
is yours of course, a present from your uncle Fred.
It's nice that we're still friends. I still can't think
what you can see in *her*. She's still so young, Sue.

Dear Jane, September now, and autumn's nearly here.
It's sad about your dad. I loved him dearly once.
The doctor says I have a lump. Don't fret. I'm sure
it's nothing serious. I feel OK. A goodnight kiss
to little Annie, and of course the tortoise and
the cat. Must go now. All love always, Mum.

A K S Shaw

GRANNY'S PICTURE

The picture on the wall
Of Granny standing tall
With her snow white pinny
Long black skirt and boots,
How I love that picture
As I love her too
Guess Grandad took the picture,
He had that kind of flare
Made her look so elegant
And wouldn't use the chair.
The background was so lovely
With roses round the door,
The thatch on the roof looked new,
The harebells were lovely blue
Reminds me of days in the country.
Days when the sun always shone
And traps pulled by ponies
Would pass down the lane,
Or the milk cart with Dobbin
Always knowing where to stop,
And Joe with his 'Good morning'
How many pints today from the churn?
Got to feed up the youngster, 'How about eggs?'
Oh, these thoughts all pass through my mind
When I look at the picture on the wall
And remember Granny and her love
That fills my heart.

Phyllis Wright

THE WAR ROOM

Voices thundered with passion,
I, I, I!
The Prime Minister's ears hurt with thoughts, theories and hate.
Scathing one man's voice boomed above all others
General Hoyden's menacing personality erupted.
'Prime Minister we must launch now
Any delay will be catastrophic.'
For a rare second, silence came
But when Hoyden ran out of words
Like a spluttering engine
The voices lifted again in unison.
'Prime Minister, Prime Minister.'
Slowly and deliberately
One man stood from his chair unnoticed.
His bright blue eyes looked around the war room
Deep into the hearts of his companion's elect.
Disorder, confusion, fear evaporated
In their place an uneasy silence descended.
The blue eyed man raised his hand smiling.
'Prime Minister, I can make this right,'
His words so rounded and soft they all listened,
If he had told them snow was hot they would have believed him.
This was the moment,
The Anti Christ made himself known to man.

Paul Willis

THE SADDEST SPRING

Funeral pyres burn, lighting the sky,
Unpleasant stench as acrid smoke billows.
In your mind's eye you see the sad eyes,
Innocent animals, slaughtered before time.

Across the bridge, fields stretch away
As far as the eye can see, but all are silent.
A lone blackbird sings a sad lament,
Spring passes unheralded, tears fall unchecked.

Joan Hopkins

THE SPEAR CARRIER'S APPRENTICE

My name is Kit Marlowe and
I am the spear carrier's apprentice.
It is a lowly task but
I carry it out with Gusto
who incidentally is
my best friend.
I believe him to be Italian.
He is certainly quite dark
and frequently smells of Garlic
who incidentally is
my black cat.
I believe him to be
Neutered. He is certainly quite dark
and frequently smells of mice
these he brings me as corpses
as I strut my stuff off-stage.

One day I shall make the leap (tights willing)
to spear carrier number one
then I'll show the groundlings
how a spear should be carried
with great élan and style
on my face a winning smile
and on my back a sign that
says he never married . . .

Dai Blatchford

GRANDAD

We didn't want you to leave us on Easter day,
Although deep in our hearts we knew you could not stay.
You fought a brave battle, right up to the end,
We missed you departing, so our love we could not send.
We rushed to be by your hospital bed,
But arrived just too late, and were told you were dead.
The family all stood hugging and crying,
Crowding round Nan for support and some loving.
I came to your side and held your hand,
My brother Ricky, not too close would he stand.
A nurse said, 'It's nearly time to go,'
We turned to leave you, hearts full of woe.
Ricky left us and he rushed to your bed,
With his skinny arms, he cradled your head.
'I love you Grandad,' were his sobbing cries,
And the tears began to run freely from his eyes.
Aunts and uncles gathered to try their best,
To explain to Ricky that Grandad's at rest.
Your funeral was a cold, wet day,
At Empshott Church, where you asked to lay.
All of us, your grandchildren walked behind your hearse,
Then silently passed to find our pew in the church.
Dad cuddled Mum and I cuddled Rick,
The service seemed to be over ever so quick.
When it was time to put you in the ground,
The sheep in the park, started to gather round.
The vicar proceeded to say a few words,
But with all the sheep bleating his voice could not be heard.
No one can explain the sheeps' behaviour that day,
But to me it was as if they knew who you were,
Their retired old shepherd, going away.

Kayleigh Rhodes (15)

THE RUFUS STONE

Hampshire's New Forest is a place of renown,
With its variety of trees rich with colour,
The forest was known as a royal hunting ground,
Used by kings one after another.

The forest was created, and thought of by William the Ist,
William the Conqueror is how he was known,
He loved to ride, and hunt in the forest,
And regarded the place as his own.

When William the 1st died his favourite son became king,
William Refus by name that was he,
Then tragedy struck while he was out hunting,
When an arrow killed him, then bounced off a tree.

William Rufus was killed by Sir Walter Tyrell,
Was it an accident, or murder, who could tell,
But his young brother Henry right away seized the throne,
Leaving poor William Rufus at the place where he fell.

Then some kind peasants lifted the body,
And onto a cart did him lower,
Taking the King from the forest to Winchester,
Where he was buried beneath the Winchester Tower.

Many years later a stone was erected,
By a gentleman named Earl De la Warr,
To mark an historic event that would not be forgotten,
A monument that would stand for evermore.

That monument is well known as The Rufus Stone,
Near Minstead is the place where it stands,
Said, to mark the spot where King Refus was killed,
Was it an accident, or a murder well planned?

Maud Eleanor Hobbs

THE STAR PRINCESS

The princess of the stars, sprinkles diamonds in the skies.
Riding her carriage of clouds, 'cross the world she flies
Throwing clusters of light along the Milky Way,
And all the constellations, glitteringly play.
Sparkling and dancing, twinkling with delight.
While the moon, her mother, shines the queen of the night.
Such visions of beauty we see everywhere,
Millions of light years away, and yet just there.
Almost at times, we could touch them it seems,
Those shafts of moonlight and silvery beams.
Calling, drawing us up to the beautiful night sky,
Our imagination takes wing, as our spirits touch and fly.

Charles F H Ruddick

CHANCE TO BELIEVE

As my body was broken
just as I feel old,
and thought I could not carry on.
With hope and desire
you are the one to help me carry on,
all I want is to stay in love with you
after everything we have been through.
It makes me want to try
deep in my soul, I know where to be,
you believe in me.
When the music begins to fade,
and colours turn grey,
I have a chance to believe
you came and answered my prayer.

Steve Wright

EMBRACE OF THE SEA

The sea appears quiet
and so gentle today,
As the tide sweeps slowly
into the bay.

Watch the warm water
softly lap the shore,
Like man seeking woman
with desire and 'amor'.

An intimate touch
then retreating again,
Soft ripples, a sigh,
shy approach, not shame.

High tide is arriving
as waves cover stones,
Gently enveloping
not resisting, she moans.

Now the passion is rising
the wind a deep roar,
Great seas are pounding
eagerly embracing the shore.

This is not in anger
but natural - the pace
At times strong and rapid,
then slowly, with grace.

With the ebb tide, sweet calm,
tranquil moon in space,
Waves sensuously kissing
the pebbles' smooth face.

Moyle Breton

CORNISH COASTS

The rugged coasts that Cornwall boasts in winter are cruelly wild,
For steely rocks bear all the knocks waiting for springtime mild.
Their colours grey from seas white spray deafening to the ears,
While high on crag we watch tides drag, shingle like washed tears.

The tension grips as rock edge slips, 'Stay back' the sea impels,
A fiery bowl to grip the soul, this scene of wildest spells.
The violent squall changes all and the screaming seagulls know,
It's time to fly through the battling sky, then stay inland and fly low.

The fiery storm after time has worn, it's violent rage declines,
The ships on waves see dead sailor's graves, exposed cruelly
                                                    by the brine.
Only those so brave who wrestle high wave, pray this wrath will desist,
For terror grips the little ships, for they're warning signs are missed.

When all goes calm we see no harm has come to those so bold,
They thank the Lord that they're prayers were heard when those
                                                    roaring seas, rolled.
How can we know what happens so, safe mortals here on land,
These storming waves are for the brave, which only sailors understand.

Lucy Bloxham

SEPTEMBER 2001

If tenderness was drowning hate
And Earth stood close to heaven's gate
With love triumphant, in the street
This world and paradise would meet.

If we could all be true to God
And go where saints and angels trod
Then we would see all human eyes
Reflecting souls where beauty lies.

If Eden's garden was regained
No evil ones on Earth would reign
And there would never be fanatics
Assembling bombs in dreary attics.

Instead of rockets, bombs and mines
I wish the light of peace would shine
We'd be like kings and queens with crowns
If all the weapons were laid down.

Phil McLynn

RIVER DREAM

I'm sitting by the river, watching the boats go by
Some are small, some are large, hey!
What do I now see? A very big barge,
I wonder, what does it carry? Where does it go?
That's something I will never know,
But my thoughts, will take me along the way
I imagine, crossing the channel,
Landing in exotic places
Eating exotic foods, then away again
To another port of call,
Will I see people in their native dress?
Joining in their night life,
Dancing away the hours until dawn
Watching the sun rise instead of setting
What a wonderful dream-world I'm creating
In my mind I'm still debating
Shall I go on or come down to earth, then
I open my eyes, I'm still sitting by the river
Watching the boats go by.

Olive Wright

CORNISH SANCTUARY

He lay on the sand in the early morning mist;
Hungry, cold and full of despair;
His mother somewhere out at sea
Separated from him in the wild autumn storm.
His white coat stained with blood
Where the cruel Atlantic waves
Had thrown him against the jagged rocks.
The night had been so dark and cold,
He had been so afraid and weak.
His round black eyes were full of tears
When he remembered how it was.
Now the tide was receding and the sun
That filtered through the mist warmed him a little.
Was this the end? Or might he yet be found?
It must be soon he knew, his life was waning fast.

Then he heard voices, and gentle hands
Lifted him carefully off the sand,
Into a box and carried him up the beach.
Soon he was at the sanctuary, where
People spoke to him kindly, treated his wounds,
Gave him food to eat and a safe place to sleep.
He was so tired, so dreadfully tired,
But now he could relax because he was safe.
This was a good place to be, he knew.
He would be made well again and when the time was right
He would be taken back to the beach, to the sea
Which was his rightful home.
He would join the other seals, like him, who had been
Made well again by this wonderful place.
The Seal Sanctuary at Gweek.

Ann Linney

TIME - HOWARTH CAR PARK

Washing, drying, hung above the cobbles in the back lane of the
cottages basking high on the hill
Shopkeepers placing their baskets of wares outside their shops to attract
the tourists which are coming down the cobbled street
To walk up and down the well-worn steps to the shops
Forever hopeful to spot a bargain
'Have you any horse shoes?' an old crippled lady asks one shopkeeper
'I've made a special trip to get them - I decorate them with lace and
pearls and give them to wedding couples for good luck I don't charge,
just give them away.'
A brief piece of her long life
She continues on her way to find the horse shoes
The heavy panting of hot dogs being walked down the hot cobbles
The click of coins in pay meters
The rev of an engine
The jackdaws still calling in the church yard whilst the blue and gold
face of time in the clock tower presides over the cobbled town
The walk of men in leather shoes on the cobbles
The click, click of high heels on the cobbles of ladies chattering,
out for the day
The tired, weary tramp up the steps of an older man
Whilst the pigeons fly overhead their wings sounding in the breeze
The black and white cat moves between The Tourist Information
and The Parsonage
He embraces the strokes with purrs of delight
His time is his own wherever pleasure is with a stroke
The sun beats down on two old ladies wondering if they have to pay
because they are disabled
The breeze carries the noise of time passing

Hilary Jean Clark

THE SOUNDS OF CORNWALL

I hear the cries of weeping gulls in the sky mourning for their
ancestors as they drift to and fro in their everlasting search.
I hear the hissing and snarling of mountainous seas as they vent
their fury against the unyielding scowling cliffs.
I hear the resonant drumming of winter rains on granite rocks
as I walk the paths in blissful solitude.
I hear the whine of constant gales as they whip the headlands
in their endless travels.
I hear the cracking grasses as my footsteps crush the hard frost
on a clear, bright winter morning.
I hear the ghostly voices of fishermen drifting eerily towards me
through the wavering sea mist on the breathless air.
I hear the fluting skylark as it spirals joyfully upwards high
into the blue canopy that stretches forever above me.
I hear the excited laughter of the silver-tipped streams
as they play their tumbling games over the sparkling waterfalls.
I hear the enveloping silence in the many dells hidden among
the steepest valleys full of strange secrets.
I hear the whispers of ancient spirits echoing through the craggy hills
as they enter the darkness of my subconscious and imprison me forever
in this primeval land, the land of which dreams are made.

Paddy Jupp

ONE LESS TOMORROW

One more candle blown,
Another year gone by,
Seventy-one birthdays,
No more than a sigh.

Yesterdays disappearing
Quickly way out of sight,
Passing so stealthily
Like thieves in the night.

Seven decades of memories,
Each one so clear,
Now fewer tomorrows,
Yet I have no fear.

I'll enjoy to the last
What life has to give,
Thanking God for His care
As long as I live.

Pat Heppel

A RELATIVE

She was blind, Micky's wife,
Humble in her ways,
Her daily life was filled with strife,
She must have seen better days.

Living in such poverty,
She was happy and content,
Shunning all society,
On honest ways her heart was bent.

Her rare enjoyment was a gin,
Occasionally a port.
This she would not regard as a sin,
To a Woodbine, too, she might resort.

She was a lover of stray cats,
But would be kind to all pets.
Birds came at her window to peck,
And thereby for entrance to beg.

She died a few years ago,
Her animal friends their sadness show.
The loss has been great for everyone,
For in her humble ways she shone like a sun.

M MacDonald-Murray

ODE TO TOPSY
(In memory of Margaret's much loved pig)

Topsy was a saddle-back pig,
Who was black and white and very big,
In the field of weeds she loved to potter,
With a leg at each corner called a trotter,
Why called a trotter, I do not know,
Topsy had one speed, and that was slow!
She ate like a pig and like a pig she snored,
And for hours could laze without being bored,
Content for her laid-back way of life,
Dreaming of becoming Sebastian's wife.
Sebastian being the saddle-back boar,
Whose tusks were removed, as they curled round his jaw,
But without his tusks he would still remain,
The most desirable man in his domain!

Topsy had hair six inches long,
We tweaked one out to prove we weren't wrong,
And showed it to all who didn't believe,
Who thought it a tale we'd told to deceive,
Truly, Topsy had very long hair,
That really made everyone stare.

We loved her funny ways and little piggy grunts,
Her sleepy, twitching nose as she dreamt of truffle hunts.
She lived happy as Margaret's pet,
And won't be forgotten yet,
Topsy was a one-off, certainly unique,
Her memory is one we will forever keep.

I wish all pigs could have the life she had,
The way some pigs are kept is really very sad!

Compassion for a life from the time of the birth,
Should be a prime condition for our place on earth!

Kate Laity

GREETINGS YELLOW

Icy, empty dawn cracks
field under our feet,
stone and star
first anemone breaks silence
harmonious wind rocks cradled
branches that touch sky.

Winter's breath streams
from our mouths, our fingers
touch slender stems to earth,
we pluck flowers
yellow sunshine tightly scrolled
in papyrus.

Bending, we meet and part
company, our units grow
apace, until bunched they
lie in box neatly, head
touching, togetherness.

The field distances
into bright gold
where earlier cloud has
been withheld, before
warmed final rows still
tight enough to harvest.

Five years coming here
with you, yet alone now,
together fingers entwined
we pick/pack, parcel
and box; later we will
pack the bulbs.

T Webster

BORN IN DEVON

I count myself among the favoured few
That I was reared in Devon's lovely land;
Yet I bemoan how little then I knew
My privilege - I could not understand
How fortune smiled on me. When now I look
With older, more appreciative eyes
Upon the commonest hill or vale or brook
In Devon, I am near to paradise.

It saddens me to think how as a child
I saw so little in those moorlands wild,
How when I walked by foaming rushing brook
Or sat in sylvan, solitary nook
On Dartmoor's fringe, I was so unaware
That loveliness unparalleled was mine,
My birthright was that heritage divine.

May I be grateful to a fate that sends
Me a belated chance to make amends
For earlier indifference; henceforth
I'll never cease to love my land of birth.

Evelyn Scott Brown

BEING THERE

We have a special privilege
And live in easy reach
For when summer evenings beckon
We can nip down to the beach.

Splash a little in the water
Have a cup of tea
Soak up a bit of sunshine
Listen to the sea.

Dust off all the cobwebs
Breathe in the fresh air
Revel in the pleasure
Of simply being there.

Jeremy J Croucher

WILD NOVEMBER NIGHT

Over one of Devon's moor land hills,
On a wild November night,
The sky heavy with cloud that spills
Flurries of snowflakes white,
Driving through darkness around the bends
Striving to see what else portends.

It had been dark, but quiet, in Lee Bay,
Before reaching the height of the moors,
We had enjoyed a pleasant day
With friends, on a Lee Abbey course.
But - the night turned wild, with wind and snow,
We had long, and dangerous miles to go!

As the headlights carved, with hopeful care,
Their path through the snow that night,
Something moved - a shadowy form was there,
At the shortened edge of the light.
Quiet suddenly, launching his way across
Was an unmistakably large dog-fox!

'Look at that!' we cried, but the fox was gone
Across, through the trees on the right.
Our driver just had to carry on,
To keep us safe, on the road, that right.
But, we'd seen a glimpse of something rare,
A fox, on his way to his home and lair!

Molly Rodgers

WHILE IT'S WARM

He finds the stroke of the brush comforting.
It has a kind of rhythm of its own,
as it applies oil to canvas,
water-colour to paper.
He likes best to paint outside in summer,
with the sun on his back.
Sometimes he has to squint his eyes a little
to see what he's painting,
to get the colours, the texture, right,
but it's nice.

The brush slides back and forwards.
Sometimes he even forgets what it is
he's actually painting.
He becomes overtaken by the motion,
the movement of his arm.
It's calming, relaxing,
as he brings it down.
The results almost pale
into insignificance by comparison,
although his studio now boasts
a fairy large collection.

The standard is mixed.
He's neither bad nor brilliant,
but good enough for his own satisfaction.
That's what counts.
That's what keeps him going
through these long months of retirement,
while his wife works on,
being almost a decade younger than him.

In an hour she'll be home.
he makes a mental note
to have her tea on in time,
but first to finish his picture,
to make the most of the weather
while it's still warm.

Andy Botterill

THE GREATER LIGHT

There is a light that will not die away
From highest hills to deeps within the sea
In spite of the grey rain this winter day.

Though the gold leaves in the dark woods decay,
Though fog wreathes bare wet branches eerily;
Though wind has withered the late flowers away,

Cold silenced a small bird's last bravest lay,
The song of the bright springs that used to be
When dawn would promise more than passing day;

shades of great ships sailed across the bay
Gliding through early mist mysteriously
Out over unknown oceans far away.

Seeking the splendour that can never stay -
The world's shore dims before eternity
Like fading coasts at the quiet close of day.

Though earth is shrouded in clouds' clinging grey;
No purple hills, no green translucent sea,
No beauty seen on this bleak winter day,
There is one light that will not pass away.

Diana Momber

ON THE MOOR

Wild gorse shines gold across the moor,
Warm contrast to the autumn sky.
Distant stones of granite stand tall,
Ancient pointers to the heavens
Standing guard across the ages.
Waiting to be touched, feel their warmth,
Absorb their energy - gathered
From a thousand lifetimes and still
Inspiring our thoughts even now.
High above, buzzards glide and soar -
Effortlessly drift on wide wings,
Lazy in the afternoon sun.
Beneath our feet, wind-crisped heathers
Colour the landscape with copper,
Springy green mosses hug the ground
Silencing the steps that we tread.
Place of haven in a mad world,
Remain our constant source of peace.

Anne Lawry

THE WHITE GOOSE

Furrowing breeze in the late afternoon sunlight,
Water circling in this willow haven,
Shimmering poplars standing nearby,
As reflected sunlight glows in this elliptical water surface,
With darkened silhouettes of Canadian geese; some upturned in
                                        underwater fantasy!
While the white goose stands sentinel over them,
As the little boy and the lady look on!

Martin Norman

THE MADNESS OF PAIN

As I lay here in this hospital bed
With weird thoughts buzzing around in my head
'Will they cut me open, take pieces away
To be replaced with plastic and clay?'
Held together and stuck with glue
They're hoping to make me good as new
I don't really care at the end of the day
About bits of plastic and lumps of clay
All I want is to be rid of this pain
That's striking me down again and again
Cut it out, take it away, you must
Please, let it be turned to dust
To be blown away without a care
In amongst the cool, fresh air
And leave me once again pain-free
To get on with life and being
Just me!

Trudi James

PENWITH

The language of the landscape:
silence of the stones,
quoits, menhirs, stone circles,
Trencrom, Men-An-Tol, Lanyon,
granite, feldspar, crinoids.
Healing powers?
Romance?
Pagan past?

Jinty Knowling Lentier

WHILE THE SEED SINGS

The world's first
mass gathering of marigolds
and mums with orange faces
under the flicker-tree flames.

Burning insects tiger brilliant
on a two acre flower
where yellow has slowly exploded
pushing radiance into inkwells.

Take off your shoes
and leave
no footprints.
There will be
no further black.
Take
your black clothes, declare them penniless,
and plunge them deep
into the cotton fields
while the seed sings
of orange.

Sheila Jeffries

AFTERNOON ON DARTMOOR

Again I walk across the moor
Where thin soil clings to rocky banks
And sheep graze short the toughened grass
Up to the foot of Crockern Tor.

Vast sky is filled with lowering cloud,
Stunted trees lean, bending low,
A swirling mist creeps slow, beyond,
All-enfolding like a shroud.

Nature seems to pause to grieve,
A frightful sadness fills the hour.
Sun-warmed climes may call - but yet,
My heart might break if I must leave.

Peg Ritchie

COOL SOFT SHADE OF POLISHED RAGS

Sit on the fence don't exhale too fast
Because the wind's going to drag you down, pull you clean under
Steal you swiftly away
Like a dreamer
Descends
Fast to this special place you rearrange your make-up
Drag on traces of a face
Once raw, honest, a prize fighter
Now worn as a boot polished rags in a garage
Box of spider webs
All I am is aware.
Aware of a fear that in each house
Behind ever blinking curtains or numb garages
We are all about to break, just split in two
China dolls of life not forming a path
Or a spectacular graph but rather
Just howling wind as an air raid siren,
A homeless mangy dog by the banks of a river,
A baby born into this world
Ready to depart to the next;
Born then writes its autobiography
In the nurse's arms,
Woman blood
And sanitised fingertips
Lightly touching.

Simon Brown

UNTITLED

King of glory, king of kings,
Beneath the shadow of the wings,
Let my oft-anxious soul abide -
Close to thy heart and wounded side

Thou alone can heal and save
With great compassion never ending -
Christ who left the lonely grave.
All our fears of death transcending

Here, alone, 'ere day is born
I kneel to thee with humble praise -
My heart sometimes so lost, forlorn
Now prayers of thankfulness shall raise

Great shepherd of the wandering sheep
The one and only Son of God -
Thy angels guard us while we sleep
Thine is the spectre and the rod.

Such solace from the Dove of peace,
From Christ who conquers sin and strife -
In the hollow of His hand
We'll find His gift the Bread of Life.

To Father, Son and Holy Ghost,
The Deity of three in one,
We offer silent hymns of praise,
For our redemption Christ has won.

Eternal Father, guard us, lead us
Through our journey here on earth -
Remove fear from death's only portal
From thee we'll gain our second birth.

M Pellow

THE BIRTH OF AN OPAL

The sunbeam loved the moonbeam,
And follow her high and low,
But the moonbeam fled and hid her head,
She was so very shy.

The sunbeam wooed with passion,
Ah, he was a lover bold
And his heart was a fire with mad desire
And oh, that fate would annihilate
The space that lay between!

Just as the day lay pointed
In the arm of twilight dim,
Then sunbeam caught the one he sought
And drew her close to him.

But one of his warm arms started
And stirred by love's first shook
She sprang, afraid, like a trembling maid,
And hid into niche of a rock.

And sunbeam followed and found her,
And led her to love's own feast,
And they were wed on that rocky bed,
And the dying day was their priest

And! The beautiful Opal
That rare and wondrous
Where the moon and sun into one,
Is the child was born to them.

Marion Susan Cornbill

EMERALD EYES

Deep within the shallow sockets
Lays like a diamond betrothed to I
Intense and energetic, I wear it in a silver locket
Days like moonlit months searching my aspirated sigh

Exotic and emerald, encased in my memory
Upon my bare chest, always waiting am I
Watching water and tide, the endless sea
Magnetic to my passion I wear an alluring eye

Everlasting envy of these two green jewels
My affection placed in an eternal lie
Impossible dream, it seems the bluest flame is cruel
This image will hold me until I die

Heart holds each eye
I incessantly cry

Danielle Collins

IF

If I were an owl I would sit in a tree
And swoop down at night when I could see
The scurrying field mice dive for cover
Squealing loudly to one another.

I would grip the branch of a sturdy oak,
And sing my song with a husky croak,
Preen my feathers of white and grey
Then flap my wings and fly away.

Ela Fleming

CITY OASIS

A walk in the woods,
A bright crisp day
Sun filters through trees
Casting shadows on leaves
The dog at my side runs to chase
A squirrel who darts for branch
Startled a bird adds his song
All is peaceful, I amble along

A chilling sound pierces the air
A siren is wailing, I remember despair
Devon's nuclear base less than a mile
Monday's practise, I thankfully smile
On tarmac ribbon, just over the hill
Cars on the way to cross the bridge
Plymouth's sculpture of concrete and steel
Cornwall's gate

The air that I breathe does not betray
The council tip just yards away
Remnants of life scattered on earth
Food half-eaten, worn-out clothes
Yesterday's treasure rusting and holed
It's all so near and yet so far
I look around and for a moment forget
That man's creations surround
God's little acre.

Sheila J Holmes

153

DANCERS

'O gentle place;' too sweet the breeze,
That languid sings and stirs each branch'ed aisle,
Of low, regretful sighs its song,
Laments your legions; unsung dreams a while.
Humming, sadly, the long forgotten lyrics of life's tragic opera to the
gentle insistent rhythm of some silent orchestra,
Whilst an unseen maestro softly marks time to the scarce remembered
tempo of a multitude of long stilled hearts.

Soft! Tender shades, as zephyrs whirl,
And tempt the twirling leaves their steps confide,
To loving, touch life's cheek once more,
Forgotten dancers; soundlessly they glide.
Turning patiently their slow, reverential waltz; 'neath sombre
sepulchral tree tops bent deferentially in prayer,
Silently they dance into eternity along leaf slicked avenues;
wet slate-grey with the burden of a million stolen tears.

Blessed tranquil plot, what treasures hide,
What unfilled dreams your wood bound vaults encase?
Yet sorrow, mellowed, sips as wine,
No acid sting to taint this poignant place.
As guileless as a child's embrace, this tear-washed gentle soil tends
them still; close and tender as any mother's bosom,
While 'neath each moss clung market abandon now, the dust-spat
bottles of a unique vintage; to oft but half supped.

'O gentle place;' this tide of blooms,
Whose scents disguise this furtive vale of grief,
Each watered with a loved one's tears,
To dew the night spun cloak of death . . . *The thief.*
Yet love 'tis fills the grieving heart's tortured cup to overflow;
that spills and wets this kind and sacred earth,
Wherein, humbled in their mortality and pressed cheek by jowl
with eternity, all men lie equal; remembered each, not for the
price of their shoes . . .

'but for how well they danced!'

Sullivan

PRECIOUS

Here's to the lady who gave me life
A doting mother and a wonderful wife
Early to bed and early to rise
Does this make our mothers wise
There's no one in the world quite like my mum
Even though she's got me instead of a son
She enjoys a laugh and her glass of gin
But not enough to make her sing
Reading books and crosswords she does by the score
When those are finished she's after more
You can't keep a good woman down or so it is said
And now I've finished this poem I'm off to bed
So here's to the lady that's my mum
A wise old bird and still full of fun.

J Snowsill

BIRDS

Over my garden electric cables pass by:
Ugly, black against a beautiful sky.
Unloved, unnoticed, almost wished away.
Until in September they have their day,
When on them the swallows gather.

Preparing to leave us, the birds chatter:
Their heads all pointing one way;
Tails streaming out behind.
Brave little birds, soon to leave us,
Flying an incredible journey far away.

And us humans? We can but sit,
Awaiting the day they come back,
To bring us summer once again.

Linda Young

SOME THINGS YOU NEVER GET OVER

It still feels like Thatcher's Britain
Well it does down our way
And I still feel the same
As I did before we had a cup of tea

And I still feel the same
As I did when I broke down

Some things you never get over
Some things you never get over

It still feels like Thatcher's Britain
Well it does down our way.

Geoffrey Downton

ALWAYS THERE

Down through the portals of time
I have heard and seen the pantomime
I was there at every turn
I have seen the planet burn

I have watched man's evolution
Seen the death and destruction
While pestilence and plaque were rife
I have watched man in such strife

I have witnessed atrocities beyond compare
Oh yes my friend, I have been there
I myself have gorged and fed
On these around me that were dead

I have watched the torturer at work
His vile game he did not shirk
I have heard the endless screams
Have smelt the blood, known what it means

I have seen the bodies cast inside
The graves of thousands man's tried to hide
I have seen the hunger, pain and death
Smelt the murderer's foul breath

The camps, the cities, the countries
I have no boundaries
All this I have seen and much more
For I am the fly upon the eternal wall.

Jeanette Jackson

ROCK POOL

A small breeze ruffles the surface
Shattering the waving life below,
Then subsides.
Slowly, rouged and emerald weeds take shape again,
Their rippling fronds stirring slightly.
From beneath a grey-smooth pebble
Sideways steps a bright green crab,
Daintily picking its way across the floor
Of this miniature ocean, intent on reaching its goal -
A decaying dogfish, left by a thoughtless fisherman
Careless of life.
Two jet-tipped hat pins peer out
From an abandoned whelk shell,
The hermit has a new cell
And is safe.
Lazy periwinkles move across the wet surface of rocks,
Browsing bovines in a seaweed meadow.
Above the waterline, sea anemones squeeze into jellied rounds
Patiently waiting for the tide to turn.
Whilst happier brethren unfurl in their warm bath beneath,
Tentacles lifting hopefully in anticipation.
Plastic prawns dart from shadowed caves
Chasing the cautious crab to the feast.
Limpets pitch their pyramidal tents tenaciously in grooves,
Nibbling at mossy algae.
I drop a stone.
They disappear -
To reform, whilst I walk away.

Diana H Adams

COMMONS TIME

I dreamed a dream of Torrington
Of thirty years ago
Where we picnicked with the children
Sweet lullaby and low

While the baby slept the afternoon
Her brothers fought a war
With sticks among the bracken
Black-bruised a grass-snake's lore

Her sister gathered flowers
Speedwell and Celandine
And laid them by the infant
Oh communion cup divine

Sheep safely grazed on Commons land
By rights this town affords
From bounteous liberality
Bestowed by ancient lords

Echoes down the ages
Of Royalists rendezvous
Of fires, chance and intended
A warmth of déjà vu

Centuries of Commons
I dream then all as one
A thousand ages in their sight
Are like an evening gone

V Jean Tyler

A FRIENDSHIP

Alone she sat, on most days now to view the sea, and dream,
The seat was on the esplanade and best to see the scene.
A widow of many years she spent lonely nights and days,
She rested there when shopping, settled in methodic ways.
He walked his dog, a daily chore, the only pal he had
Along the seafront walking fast, as always, from a lad.
He saw the woman on the seat, he nodded a good day
She smiled and said, 'Good morning,' he went on his way.
Passing by and smiling the many weeks went by
Until he saw an empty seat which made him wonder why,
Of course he asked where she had been, 'Unwell for just a while,'
He walked home slowly, thinking, how much he liked her smile.
Need I say more about these two? Friends, not lonely now
Yes, it led to deeper things, you know why and how.

Patricia Evans

THE TRANSFORMATION

Dusk teeters on the edge of darkness,
Birds have sung their final song,
Stars appear to cheer the darkness,
And whisper that nightfall will not be long,
The watchful moon spins silver beams
Across the sleepy sky,
And nightfall inches slowly,
Drawing ever nigh,
Indi go fades to charcoal,
The transformation is complete,
And the earth below grows weary,
And closes its eyes, to sleep.

Clare Allen

THE MILLENNIUM BOBBY

Domestic violence in the home
Rape, abuse, paedophilles roam
Burglary, theft, robbery
Scenes of crime, paperwork for me.
RTA, fire and flood
Injury, fatality, the sight of blood
Mugging, assault and road rage
Cameras watching, the modern phase
Crowd control, riot and drug raid
Teamwork, will overtime be paid?
Hostage, missing person and suicide
Negotiators with a caring side
Helicopter, dog handler and mounted patrol
Mobile, static or out for a stroll.
Trespass, vandalism and criminal damage
Done by a careless rampage
Noisy parties and alarm
Keeping the peace, possible calm
Mentally ill, psychiatric report
Absconding bail, custody and court
Juveniles and pimps giving orders
Runaways sleeping in shop corners
CS gas, body armour and baton
With armed officers frowned upon
Evidence, witness and signed page
Too light a sentence, public outrage.

I couldn't do it,
Could you?

K Cook

My Awareness

We must learn to forgive and to forget
The decisions we come to make should
                    hold no regrets

The things that were said and done to us in our past
If we remember this hurt only the bitterness will last

What higher power dictates right from wrong?
Society and the belief have made the rules for so long

Judgmental the human race has come to be
But the insight to understand is hard to see

We go through life not realising or seeing we are all
                                    destined to decline
Man is so insignificant in the evolution of time

Our thoughts and the ability to show compassion we feel
This has developed due to our ancestors and been instilled

Will people in the future continue to be compromised?
If war, hate and resentment is allowed to enter their lives.

Anthony Ross-Fallon

Friendship

No need to see each other every day,
every week, every month.
Our friendship is stronger than that.
We each know we are there for one another.
If either of us needed the other,
we would be there.

Pam Stevens

162

OUTBACK PAINTER'S COMPOSITION

Smeared from the palate, this sky, beyond the eye
to sky below, fallen on the water's flow;
broken by the flurried stroke of brush,
drifts us to the ashen boundaries
of a man's anguished bewildered world
captured in colour.

A landscape from the origins of man,
span our horizon.
End to end are dead trees, rooted on a sullen
soil whose only harvest is skeletal.
Lizard-like, a metaphor crawls its way
Across a falling angel with a devil's head.
Dead this work, dead.
The Horn of Plenty already drained
by thirsty creatures
straining to chain their images upon his mind.
Yellow bird, two-headed torture, black-beaked
unkind struts by the shore of a dying sea.
Sulphur smothers the senses, erases calm
as a serpent sheds a double rainbow;
lack-lustre legend in Aboriginal lethargy.
Dragged across his unending desert,
Dust thick on our skin from the dreary smudges
of his interpretation, we find no oasis.
Only an Australian longing to go back again,
beyond
the Song of Solomon and a primitive beginning
to a sky behind a sky.

Janine Vallor

EVENING OVER THE ISLES OF SCILLY

Glimpses of pink behind dark clouds,
White wisps mottle the blue sky,
The swell of the ocean . . .
Calm and steady.

A few lone herring gulls fly over
Still searching . . . still scavenging,
Cormorants wing their way . . . looking for fish.

A bell peals its sonorous message
Gloomy . . . foreboding,
Two lighthouses flash out their beams
Warning ships to stay away.

Across the water . . . St Agnes
A long low island
A few solitary homes.
Beyond . . . rocks . . . strewn all round,
Stretching on and on . . .

These magical islands
Surrounded by water,
Joined by the constant to and fro of boats,
Skippered by seasoned boatmen,
Their craft handed down
Over many generations.

It feels like
Another time . . . another place
In these furthest reaches of the British Isles.

Gerald Conyngham

RAYMOND

Raymond was a man of honour,
His nature unassuming,
Perfection was his keyword
And nothing else would suit him.

He was adept with his camera
Many prizes did he win.
Raymond was a quiet old stick
But he always met you with a grin.

He liked to sail the estuary
In his beloved yacht,
In and out the many creeks,
All cares and worries forgot.

He loved his family dearly
And how proud they were to go
With him to the Palace
To receive his I.S.O.

He bore his illness bravely
Though often in great pain.
But now he is sleeping peacefully
Never to feel pain again.

Now that you are parted
He will never be far away,
For he will be watching over you
Each night and every day.

Phyllis Ing

REVIEWING THE SITUATION

When putting on my make-up
I've noticed the slightest change.
Could it be my face has dropped
Perhaps it's just my age.

It could be that bit firmer,
So I'll use a bit more cream -
But it may not make me younger,
For I know I'm not sixteen.

I'd thought about the none-surgical face-lift,
And wondered 'Would that work?'
But would the wrinkles really shift?
I'm really not too sure.

Maybe if I massage it gently,
And get my eight hours sleep -
It may not get too wrinkly -
Then my looks - I may just keep.

For when I'm walking down the street,
Some people look much worse -
Could be they've left things much too late,
So I'll let things take their course.

Many sagging chins I've seen,
And crows-feet by the score -
Jowls and orange-peely skin,
So mine I could ignore.

Especially as people may think I'm vain
And my looks I shouldn't save -
For I can't be forever a girl in teens -
When I've just turned fifty-five.

Wendy Watkin

BEAUTY

Out of the ground comes the river
A tiny slow trickling stream
Sees the sun and the grass, a small insect
Incredibly lovely they seem

Carving a way through a meadow
It's stronger and wider and deep
Sees a horse gentle cows, little fox cubs
A tiny new lamb with the sheep

Gurgling on over boulders
By flowering sweet smelling weeds
In the shallows a bird is just bathing
A swan has its nest in the reeds

Above it the sun makes it sparkle
Below it fish swim silver gold
Round an island that's safe for all wildlife
Mature rushing strong, proud and bold

All of this beauty sustaining
It's there, part of nature's great plan
It developed and grew and existed
Was there since the world first began

Artists put nature on canvas
With talent respect and restraint
But compared with the grandeur of nature
It seems like a small dab of paint.

Enid Gill

THE WINDS OF TIME

I am a leaf, borne on the winds of time.
In the springtime, I formed as a bud,
Firmly fastened to the blossoming tree,
And I grew in my summer days to a rich and ripening fullness.
In the first darkening days of autumn,
My colour fading, my form diminishing,
I broke forth from the tree in a whirlwind of confusion -
Free at last, but still captive to the vagaries of the winds,
The breath of the breeze, the hurly-burly of the hurricane,
I am yet carried onward, forward, sometimes downward -
Rarely still;
A slave to the might of the gale,
An unchained prisoner of the winds.
I am swept up and down at random -
No will -
No direction -
No senses -
No source of nurture now -
But with a growing exhilaration born out of the unforeseen,
The charting of, for me, hitherto uncharted ways -
An excitement of discovery.
There is nothing to hold me, or restrain me -
No sheltering branch or bole.
The whole universe lies ahead,
Once the winds and the earth have claimed me, changed me . . .
And I, them.

Jenny Proom

FOSSIL FOREST AT LULWORTH

What moved the earth when you were green?
Were birds amongst your branches seen?
Did wolf and bear in forests find
The lairs which men had left behind?
Did early man to cave life turn
Flint knives to kill, wood fires to burn?
And slowly, slowly, as you grew
Was naked land possessed by you?
You fossil trees, the sea beside,
Did Ice Age fell you in your pride?
Leave of your lives these stony rings,
Teach Lulworth Cove of ancient things?
Hunters and farmers passed you by
When metal tools they learnt to ply.
The sea withdrew and left you there;
From tide to tide your shapes were bare.
I wonder, did their children play
With stone and sling in David's way?
Did they, so early, choose their king
For prowess with the stone and sling?
And will such fossil fragments stay
When man the killer's brought to bay?
Will shattered towers and fallen dome
Tell where, long since, we made a home?
And when our race is growing old,
Will you still show your rings of gold?

Kathleen M Hatton

CUP OF LOVE

My auntie lived beside the sea
she lived with my grandma and me.
The magic of the sun and sand
the memory of the tender hand.
Picnics in the countryside
picking bluebells that soon died.
Life was good and love was there
each time I needed gentle care.
As years passed by and I grew up
I needed to drink from the cup
of memories of happy years
to stop the pain and dry the tears.
And now I sit beside the bed
and gently stroke the little head
of beauty sleeping warm and snug
and know she'll wake up to a hug.
I'll take her hand and walk the way
my auntie took me to the bay.
I'll stack her memory full of plenty
and fill her cup so it's never empty.

Brenda Weir

ALWAYS THE WOODS

Whenever I go into the woods
it's in search of something inside me
that, like a tune, evades all my words
and, like a tune, lightens and weighs me -

that elegy of childhood sunlight
scalloped in a languid garden leaf,
the flowerhead that never knew late
but had the earliness of a laugh.

And, though I go there late and with
cloud muting the tune, I find hair-grass
sparks in my hand like a spring's breath.
Surely it is the tune's earliness.

And the sky's sulk and the north-west wind
worry the trees to a water's dance -
like my skin, so I am weighed, lightened
and lifted by that flash of oceans.

Chris White

YOU AND I

When you grow old, will you want me there,
Will we still have a life, that we can share.
When you grow old will your love remain,
Will our hearts still sing the same refrain.
When you grow old, will I have your heart
Like I've always had it, right from the start.

When I grow old I'll want you there,
Though you may be stooped, and have thinning hair.
When I grow old, it must be with you,
Then we can talk, of the things we've been through.
When I grow old, I will love you more,
Than I ever did, in the years before.
When I grow old, will you love me too,
Will you need me as much as I need you.

When we grow old, will we still explore,
The country roads, and the open moor.
When we grow old, will our minds remain,
Shall we still sing, love's old refrain.
When we approach the very end,
I'll still have you, my love and my friend.

D Marriott

NELLY

As she fell from the swing
The elastic went ping!
An 'er draws wer' down round 'er legs,
The boys all laughed
An 'er friends and best girlfriends all pointed and jeered,
Which brought Nelly to 'er knees in tears.

As she made 'er way 'ome
Shouting, 'Leave me alone!'
Clutchin' draws, elastic and shame,
Young 'Arry who she liked
Said, 'Nelly, it's alright,'
As he ran wiv 'er down the lane.

Now spluttering a little less,
The tears dried on 'er dress
As she sat with Arry by the lake',
For he borrowed 'er draws
An' elastic of course!
They sat fishin'
Wiv 'is arm round 'er waist.

Phillip A Taylor

AN OPEN BOOK

I wanted to learn to tango, waltz or twist and shout.
So, I went along to the library to take a dance book out.
But before I got to the section on 'Ballroom at your own pace'
I caught sight of an open book and a grin spread over my face.

The book wasn't about dancing at all
in fact, it was on hypnotism.
I wondered as I skimmed the pages
if I could *imagine* I'd got rhythm!

Well I read the book and now when I dance
I feel I'm almost in a trance.
Reading the contents my mind set did alter.
Now I *think* I'm John Travolta!

So readers if you find an open book,
take it home and have a look.
For you never know what information you'll find.
It could even improve your state of mind!

Lynn Shakespeare Branner

WHAT IS AGE?

I am a pensioner of ninety years on
But none of my faculties have gone,
I can cook and wash and iron and sew,
And sit and watch my flowers grow,
Planted by wrinkled hands
Are some of the plants from foreign lands.

Being old if you're fit and well
Is very rewarding I can tell.
My hearing being very good
I sometimes hear more than I should,
My eyesight is poor but I can see
Who comes to the door to visit me.
I can walk a while till my heart misses a beat
Then I gently stroll till I find a seat.

Age brings memories good and bad,
Both of which I've certainly had.
While life for some has just begun,
For me well, I'm ninety years young.
I thank the Lord each night when I pray
That I've been spared another day.

Muriel Johnson

A SHACKLED SONNET

It came unbidden, gentle, shy, a glance.
They hover, swarming, gnat-like somewhere near.
If thought remains, just that, don't look askance.
Like juggled balls to catch or drop my dear.
Trespassers are still visitors not guests,
Some sidle in and out again and some,
Not only leave their calling card, unrest
But mark your cards and un-invited come,
Invading quiet of sleep, rewrite the past
To forge a bond and shackle the mind with words
That slither and slip, soft chains. Come join the cast,
A girl; a smile; a poem, discordant chords
That leave their mark and come on cue to bow.
Their exit made, off stage maybe for now.

Jack Major

CHRISTCHURCH

When one first pictures Christchurch, the look can be quite sour,
For it is a very quiet spot with many a lovely bower.
To me - a Londoner by birth
The time spent there certainly proved its worth.
Not a big town like Bournemouth or Poole,
But very close knit although only small.
For you see with neighbours who are loathe to let us be,
It is very difficult to remain free.
I reside in a village on the outskirts of town,
In a little maisonette I can call my very own.
There are tributaries of the rivers Avon and Stour around,
Whose waters are very peacefully bound.

Betty Green

11TH SEPTEMBER 2001

As the news gradually unfurled
We learned of an attack upon the world.
People of every race and creed
Were subject to this atrocious deed.
Civil airliners were used to power
The felling of each World Trade Centre Tower.
Then the mighty Pentagon
Was hit by those 'Anon'.
The hijackers will serve their time in hell
Not in a very comfortable cell.
We must not forget the good
Who did all that they could
To save others lives, and themselves died;
They must all be recognised,
For *they* were nothing less than *saints*!

Catherine Blackett

YOUTH

Pomona sat late in the orchard,
Curtained by mist and dewy sheep.

Apples scattered,
Abandoned, fermenting.

An apple sliced sideways,
Revealing the pentangle.
Is this the knowledge that Athena held,
When she outwitted Hercules?

On Tir Na Nog apples lie scented.
Waiting, waiting,
For youth's first cut.

C L Buchanan-Brown

NEVER AGAIN

Let me tell you about the summer of love.
To walk around with the feeling that your soul has been ripped in two,
And that the person you love, does not love you,
Well you do not notice the season.
Rather than the season of laughter, sun, sea and sand,
The season is dull, no matter how hard the sun tries to shine.
Yet despite that there could be no other who could replace your
broken heart.
There he stood.
This was my summer of love.
He replaced my long days of misery,
Replaced them with laughter, sun, sea and sand and hope.
Without you there was no poetry in my soul,
My life was not my own,
You filled the aching, black hole,
I was no longer alone,
And never again.

Hollie Simmons

SNAKE

This true story I do undertake
is to tell you the take of an angry snake.
As I was digging in a Devon bank
to plant a daffodil
I thought I heard a hissing sound
Quite loud

and sharp
and shrill.

Peering closely at the ground
to try and trace the angry sound.
A snake's head I nearly kissed!
The startled snake stared at me
and hissed.
As I felt ready to take flight,
the grass snake slid smoothly
out of sight
into the woods of dappled light.

Kathleen Harper

POOLE WIND SPRITES

Like flocks of seabirds
Lured by storm churned shoal,
Board sailors, kite boarders
Drawn by forecast of onshore wind.
Battling the elements,
Revelling in the force of waves,
Lifting, gyrating
Wafted by wind's whim -
Riding the wave curve where the surf begins;
And the foam swamped surfboards watch . . .
Envying the glorious aerobatics
Of wind's wunderkind.
Round them, fussing sheep dogs,
The water scooters
Snarl and slide,
Bound by dependence on motors . . .
Waterborne watching the windborne,
Waveborne freedom of those
Offshore visitors
To Poole.

Di Bagshawe

A LOWER LATITUDE

In some shielded minor space
A fallen floor beneath greater plains
Where, upon its axis, I spin
Where hysteria is all I hear
Its guideless tones - a paradox,
Never a safer state
Of equanimity: prone to confusion
And settle for distraction.

Does the light which travels down
Reflect off the mirrors that surround?

The breathing stills and the hour is replaced
By zero. Save me now!

In this motion, pictures slow
To pause,
On this open mirror shield
Elevated onto a mass exterior
Where horizons stretch - a steady path,
Where lies true equability.

Laura Lang

RESTLESS BYWAYS

Ancient byways with secrets untold,
Their hidden torment begins to unfold,
Their twists and scars are there to see,
Their dark past holds the key.

The wind's haunting melody gives a clue,
The trees close in engulfing the light,
Dread begins to fill my soul
As the chill air begins to bite.

The dead reach our across the void,
Embracing a shudder of fear,
Make haste! Make haste!
Away from.

Those dark and dismal lanes where restless spirits wander,
Spectres, ghosts and apparitions dwell,
And ghastly phantom funeral processions
Haunt to the chime of the midnight bell.

Robert Newland

NOW THERE IS ONE

When you are a couple,
You're accepted where e'er you go.
Whether on a holiday,
Or maybe to a show.

When one of the couple
Is no longer here,
Where are your lifetime 'friends'
To help you through your fears?

All of a sudden they're 'busy'
And haven't got the time.
No more coffee mornings,
To see if you're doing fine.

No one to turn to
When you're ill in bed.
To see if you need shopping
Or perhaps help to be fed.

Yes, loneliness is no bed of roses
Believe me it's no fun.
At least you know who your friends are
At the moment there are none.

Yvonne Lewis

THE DANCING

My book beckons, and the warmth of the fire
These two can give me all I desire
The wind is howling, and the wind slaps the pane
But it's time to go Scottish dancing again.
So I force myself to climb the stairs
To change my clothes, and comb my hair.

The light shines-out as I open the door
People gathered in groups all round the floor
Smiling faces call greetings from friends old and new
Now what have I done with my other shoe?
The music starts up as Joan calls 'Make a set'
Oh memory please work, don't let me forget!

A moment's panic as I try to recall
How does it begin, the start of it all?
Ah! - it's alright, Joan is going to walk-through
It's a Godsend for me, though it's boring for you.
The music is magic, you can't hold your feet
Shut the door, or we'll all dance away down the street.

Grasp your partner's hand a little tighter
With every dance our hearts grow lighter
At the end of the evening, we say fond farewells
We are pleasantly tired, and pleased with ourselves
What made me think that warmth was in fire
And that my book and my chair were all I desired?
This feeling of ease, and the comforting glow
Come from joy in the dancing with people I know.

P Henderson

AUGUST HOLIDAY

Ramble on cliff top paths I spy
The picturesque, tumbling cliffs,
Seaweed-strewn shingle,
Rugged sea views and Georgian
Seaside cottages with slate roofs.
Tide sucking on exposed sands,
Washed-up yachts in the harbour,
White, vertical masts like cuttlefish,
Lines of rigging in pencil,
Rounded, royal blue hulls,
The tide lifting boats,
Ballerinas in a dancing partner's
Arms, families picnic on soft sands.
A seagull watching the artist
Painting in gouache from the Cobb wall
A view of the charcoal cliffs,
Charmouth Museum a shell on the shore,
Mirroring the colours of nature
Upon the printing paper
Laid out across the mellow, warm stones
On an August holiday afternoon.
A girl in a linen dress throws
Rounded, wave-smoothed pebbles
In the gentle waves which wash
Stones along the foreshore,
The softness of the day enfolding her.
Ropes of brown hair unfurling
Beneath the dampness of the spray.

Janet Eirwen Smith

DECISION TIME

As I sit and ponder,
These thoughts came to me,
Shall I take a little rest,
Or go out on the spree.

After the turmoil of today,
I think the first is best,
The body at this moment,
Is not too full of zest.

While thinking where shall I go,
The sunlounger caught my eye,
And as the weather is so fine,
I'll just give it a try.

In the peace and quiet of the garden,
Just the birds for company,
An extra cushion for my head,
Plus a cake and cup of tea.

Now everything is set up,
A lying position I will take,
Enjoy the beauty all around,
And the tea and cake.

Now I'm sure my choice was right,
And I can take my ease,
Enjoy the warmth of the sun,
And only me to please.

I feel I must put the cup down,
My eyelids are closing fast,
And the thoughts of a spree,
Are way out in the past.

Will A Tilyard

SHADOWS OF AUTUMN

Evening sun
Glistens on bough
Love in the air
Children's fun

Robin on branch
Breeze lifts leaves
Peace in the air
Gives love a chance

Joy in my heart
Light in the soul
Shadows of autumn
We will never part

Wonder on wonder
Golden days coming
Joy in the heart
Love growing fonder

Whispers in valley
Berries on hedges
Shadows of autumn
On clear air carry

Dew drops on grass
Apples fall gently
Bees made honey
All things will pass

Memories of gold
That never fade
Love is in the air
There always to hold

Grace Anderson

THE AMERICA'S CUP JUBILEE

Azure sea, azure sky
Yachts like jewels in lazuli
This, a once-in-a-lifetime sight
America's cup off the Isle Of Wight.

The challenge to sailing first begun
In eighteen hundred and fifty-one
When, a squad of New York business men
Vowed to outsail the Brits - and then

Racing round the Isle of Wight
They took the cup and proved 'em right
It's 2001 - Jubilee year
The Solent's agog - everyone's here!

200 at the starting line
The sea looks good, the weather's fine
There's the Prince of Denmark, the Aga Khan
The Duke's here too where it all began.

Here's to our brothers across the sea
And the spirit they brought with the Jubilee
They've taken Cowes, just a quaint little town
Lifted her up, made her renown.

Alas, terrorists have taken our brothers to heaven
Terrorist hijackers in 707s
They ran a good race and now they have gone
But their sporting spirit will ever live on.

Norah Page

LEAVE ONLY FOOTPRINTS

Warmly clothed this crisp wintry day
Air so clean, gentle horses sit sea of grey
Chasing the waves on the clean soft sand
I walk with my dog leash in hand
As she runs and chases the ebbing tide
It's only her paw prints the sea will hide
The whispering sand says, 'Thank you please stay
You leave only your footprints when you walk away.'

Soon the warm weather change this serene scene
Cars and coaches will bring tourists and trippers
Heading for the beach to mark out their pitches
Bottles, sandwiches, cans, oil to name but a few
These items they'll bring, on the sand they will strew
Litter-bins empty too far to go, after eating their ice cream
The wrappers they'll throw, onto the sand once soft and clean -
Or into the sea hoping never to be seen.

The sun's going down but the sunset is grey
The tourist and trippers have gone for today
My heart is saddened by the troubled tide
Frothy and littered it struggles to clean
The debris left where the sunworshipper's had been
As I turn around to walk away
The whispering sands cry out and say
'Please tell these people when they leave each day
Leave only their footprints to wash away.'

Ann Marie Moseley

SCIENCE

The sun is rising and the species wakes.
The valley of the shadow falls away.
Fine people are appearing everywhere,
With minds alerts and prospects fair - there where
Science, its mighty flag unfurls flapping
In the morning air. Empirical and
Corroborated, its quest it follows
Ever closer to approximate Truth -
That Truth which is the breath of life for all.
Encourage them: stand and praise all those who
Dare the stars to question far and near with
Microscopes and telescopes, electron
Probes and radio till cancer yields and
Sickness flees - blessings for the multitudes.

The sun is rising and the species wakes.

Desmond Tarrant

THE A30 IN SPRINGTIME

The golden, billowing banks of furze,
  Bullion bountiful and free,
To delight the eye of the traveller,
  And entice the early bee.

The lacy, bridal blackthorns, shower
  Their white confetti pearls,
Like snowflakes fluttering in the breeze,
  A frosting on the nettles.

The bluebells nod their carillons,
  To adorn the hedgerow skirting,
Among uncurling bracken fronds,
  From the rust of winter bursting.

Beneath life's tinsel hazards lurk,
  Thorns and stings for the heedless,
The dolce vita takes its toll,
  The glitter concealing its falseness.

John Jenkin

FLIGHT

Borne on the uplift of another's flight
Hunting the sun, swiftly onwards they fly.
A common direction, sharing this might.

God grant to us such visionary sight
That united we may soar to the sky.
Borne on the uplift of another's flight.

Follow the formation birds in their flight
Sharing the point, as south winds whisper why?
A common direction, sharing this might.

Wings wet with raindrops jewelled catching the light.
Fill our lives with such beauty our souls sigh.
Borne on the uplift of another's flight.

Trust in each other, fly up to the heights.
As the birds, reach to that warm sun on high.
A common direction, sharing this might.

As life ebbs away and death is our plight
Stand firm together till that last goodbye.
Borne on the uplift of another's flight.
A common direction, sharing this might.

Georgina McManus

ON THE WIND

When I am gone:
Look for me on the wind;
See my shape in the shadows
Under the trees;
Hear my crunching footfalls
On the gravel of the drive;
Watch for the dint of my shoes
On the wet green of the lawn;
Learn that I have joined the birds
In their shrubbery chorus,
Praising the spring;
That I am smiling
In the blossoming of the first rose.
Always I shall be there
Watching over you
When my tangible days are done.
How could it be otherwise
When it has been my duty
And delight to care for you
Down all those years?
How could the mere sloughing of my body
Change all that?
So, and especially,
Watch for me by moonlight.
I shall be there.
Always it was our time.

Ted Harriott

TIME THAT PASSES

We only know the passing time
In history a well-known mime
On Earth in eras
Known in fears as
The clock tells the renewed story
Oft' times not of all our glory.

The truth Earth or planet as
We know it must pass
We are told
Not in the same mould
As man does plunder and exact
With each passing fury and rash act

A print of devastating proportion
Demise to the animals our portion
The sickening death to
All that grew:
While science weaves its wanton way
The sorry spectacle of terror must waylay

Aspirations and hopes renewed
For a time-place in eternity viewed.

John Amsden

HUSH LITTLE BABY

Hush little baby, don't you cry
Mummy will sing you a lullaby
Mummy will hold you warm and tight
For when you're a man you will have to fight

This world of ours is filled with fear
I wish I could always have you near
We thought we could bring peace to this earth
But there are those who think life has no worth

Hush little baby don't you cry
Maybe one day before you die
All of us in this big wide world
Will see the banner of peace unfurled

We will strive and we will try
So hush little baby don't you cry

Jenny Brownjohn